ORGANIZE NOW! A WEEK-BY-WEEK GUIDE TO SIMPLIFY YOUR SPACE AND YOUR
LIFE

ISBN: 9781796667073

Front Cover Designed by: Laura Dudek
Author Photo by: Cara Kilian Photography

First Printing: November 2010
Second Printing: February 2019 (New Revised Edition)
Printed in the United States of America

First Edition: November 2010
Second Edition: February 2019

Visit www.JenniferFordBerry.com

A DAILY PLAN

ORGANIZE
NOW!

TO SIMPLIFY YOUR SPACE + LIFE

A DAILY PLAN

ORGANIZE NOW!

TO SIMPLIFY YOUR SPACE + LIFE

VOLUME I
NEW REVISED EDITION

JENNIFER FORD BERRY

ABOUT THE AUTHOR

Jennifer Ford Berry is an expert in helping people get their life organized, clear clutter and achieve their dreams. She has written several books on this topic including *Organize Now! think and live clutter-free* and *Organize Now! your money, business, and career.* Jennifer is a passionate speaker that loves to speak to audiences all over the globe. You can also listen to her on The 29 Minute Mom Podcast.

Visit JenniferFordBerry.com for more information, organizing tips and resources. You can also find her on Facebook: facebook.com/jenniferfordberry/ and Instagram: @jenniferfordberry. Jennifer currently resides in Western New York with her husband Josh and two children.

ACKNOWLEDGMENTS

I would like to thank each and every person who has ever supported my work as an organizer or has helped turn my passion for organizing into a book.

To those friends and family members who have genuinely supported this project.

A special thanks to my parents, Randy and Linda, for teaching me that I can do anything I set my mind to.

To all of those who have allowed me into their homes, offices, and lives. It's been a privilege to help you get organized.

Finally, thank you God for your favor on this book and for blessing my life.

DEDICATION

For my children, Randsley and Bryceton, I hope this proves that if you work hard enough anything can happen. Randsley, your compassion, beauty, kindness and "old soul" makes me so proud to be your mother. Bryceton, I love your humor, strength and cuddles. You have taught me so much about the bond between mommies and sons. Sweet dreams, my loves.

And for my husband, Josh, who continuously supports my dreams and goals. Your hard work and dedication to our family amazes me. I look forward to making the rest of our dreams come true together.

contents

introduction

I have loved to organize since I was a child, but that doesn't mean it doesn't take work for me to stay organized. Even as I write this book, I am keeping up with a house, two young children, two businesses, the flood of paperwork from my daughter's school, bills, volunteer work and spending time with family and friends spread out across the country. We all have moments when we wish we could snap our fingers and have an organizing fairy arrive to put everything back in order, but the reality is that staying organized takes work.

When I started writing this book I thought I should sound like a professional organizer, but then I remembered why I wanted to write this book to begin with—I felt people needed a simple, straightforward book to help them get their lives organized. There are way too many books on the shelves that give lengthy advice, paragraph after paragraph about how to get organized. The truth is that people are strapped for time these days and just want to be told (in the quickest way possible) how to get their lives organized.

To enter the mystery of timelessness is to enter the sanctuary of the here, where we are given a chance at every moment to begin our lives again. Not one of us is perfect, and sorrows press upon us all. But, the universe is a merciful one, in which unlimited opportunities for new beginnings are built into the very essence of things.

—MARIANNE WILLIAMSON

This book will not remove the work involved in getting organized, but it will give you fast, simple and straightforward guidelines to follow and useful tips to help you stay organized for the rest of your life. As a mother of two, a wife, a business owner and now an author, I know how important time is. I promise this book will not waste your time with long paragraphs of explanation. To make the organizing process even easier, I have broken the book down into categories: Organize Yourself, Organize Your Papers, Organize Your Things, Organize Your High-Traffic Areas, Organize Your Personal Spaces, Organize Your Storage Areas, Organize Your Special Events, and Organize Your Routines.

Each week a series of small goals will be set for you. Focus on one goal until completion and then move on to the next. Remember that these are baby steps, so throughout the week move at a pace that is comfortable for you. There are a number of tips to help you reach each week's goals. If you find these tips helpful, use them. If they don't work for you, follow your own methods to reach your organizing goals. Remember, you know your organizational needs better than anyone else.

Use the book in a way that best meets your needs. You can follow the book straight through or skip around to weeks that address the biggest problem areas in your life.

My hope is that after you complete this book you will be unburdened by your clutter. By doing this I hope you find more clarity so you can see who you really are and start living your life with renewed purpose.

THE **basics** OF ORGANIZATION

Ways to Conquer the Clutter

Clutter comes in many shapes and sizes. Clutter can be debt, baggage from a previous relationship, weight gain, health issues or those stacks of papers scattered all over the kitchen counter. When sorting, always ask yourself: Do I love this? Or, do I use this? If you are tired of allowing the clutter to control your life, make a choice to L.I.V.E.

L=List. If you don't write it down, chances are you will forget it.

I=Internal Organization. Organization starts on the inside first.

V=Vision. Be very clear about the vision you have for your life, and then keep that in the forefront of your mind throughout everything you do.

E=External Organization. When you have yourself organized internally and know where you are going and why, then you can begin the task of organizing your external environment.

The Cost of Clutter

You know clutter is a bad thing, but did you ever stop to think about all of its negative effects?

- Clutter causes you to feel overwhelmed or depressed.
- Clutter robs you of your energy.
- Clutter steals 50 percent of your storage space.
- Clutter makes life harder. You have to look longer, travel farther and dig deeper to find what you are looking for.
- Clutter takes longer to clean.
- Clutter costs you money. If you can't find what you need, you buy a replacement. Or, you may be paying to store your clutter.
- Clutter makes it hard to think straight.
- Clutter may affect how you feel about yourself. You may be self-conscious or feel guilty about your clutter.
- Clutter can affect your relationships. For example, if you feel ashamed of your cluttered house, you may be less likely to invite friends and family for visits.
- Clutter takes away the peace and beauty from a home.

Organizing your life can be an overwhelming experience. But if you let clutter continue to pile up, it will drain your energy. Take a minute to try this exercise: Focus on a cluttered area in your home. How do you feel when you look at this area? Stressed? Overwhelmed? Depressed? Getting organized will help you feel better emotionally and physically.

Many people I have worked with say they don't have the energy to get organized. That is because clutter steals our energy. Clutter often starts growing when our energy is low, such as during the colder months.

> *Deciding to simplify our lives and bring order to our homes by sending on the objects we no longer love to new, happier incarnations with people who will genuinely appreciate them is the way to open ourselves up to receiving an abundance that will perfectly suit us.*
>
> **—SARAH BAN BREATHNACH**

This is why many of us use the words "spring cleaning." In the spring many of us feel recharged, full of new life and fresh beginnings. We have more energy, thus we feel the need to remove clutter from our homes and offices to make a fresh start.

Eliminating clutter and organizing your life will give you more energy, lift your spirits and make room for better things and experiences to come into your life. It's a tremendously freeing and liberating experience. You will be able to find everything you need when you need it and finish projects and tasks on schedule.

As with everything, practice makes perfect, so the more you practice organizing, the easier it becomes. Once your outer environment is clean and clear, you can focus on nurturing your inner environment and spending more time with the ones you love.

Psychology of Clutter

Getting rid of stuff is very hard for us to do. It takes time; it can be very overwhelming, and most of us never know where to start or exactly how to go about it. I happen to love change. However, I know many people who hate it—including my husband and my sister. Maybe you need help getting rid of your clutter. You need a change agent in your life. Face your fear or the shame of someone seeing your cluttered home and call a friend to help you get organized.

In her book Clear Your Clutter With Feng Shui, Karen Kingston says, "Life is constant change. So when something comes into your life enjoy it, use it well, and when it is time, let it go. Just because you own something, it doesn't mean that you have to keep it forever. You are just a temporary custodian of many things as they pass through your life."

Whether we realize it or not, we have a relationship with everything we own. Each possession connects us with specific people, events or seasons in our lives. Deciding what to toss means connecting with each object, confronting its place in our lives and deciding

The size of the average American home has nearly doubled in the last fifty years. The average income has also increased. What does this have to do with clutter? We make more money, so we spend more and buy more things to clutter up our larger houses!

what to do with it.

You probably have many different reasons for holding on to the clutter in your life. It takes courage to let go, but if we don't let go of old things, we can't make room for new things to come. Here are some common reasons for hoarding, along with arguments against them.

I JUST CAN'T PART WITH THIS...

- **Emotional attachment.** Remember, you can part with an item and still keep the memories.
- **Status and security.** Feng shui teaches that your thoughts create your future. If you get rid of something thinking you will need it again as soon as you throw it away, chances are that's what will happen! But if you are aware of this, you can stop it from happening. Trust that if you need this item in the future the universe will provide a better version.
- **Advertisers say you need it.** Our society is constantly bombarded with messages from advertising companies that say we need this and we need that. And what is worse, they make us believe that if we don't get it we will be less. So we buy more and more. Next time an ad gives you the urge to buy something, stop and ask yourself if this item will be used continuously or if it will bring you joy for more than two months. If you answer yes to one of these questions, it may be worth purchasing. If not, you will probably forget all about it in a week. Owning things does not always make us happy. Shopping can give us a rush, but long-term happiness is something no product can give us.

- It's how you were raised. You may have been taught by a parent to hang on to things. This is all the more reason to clear the clutter from your life so that you can be a good example to your own children.
- The mess is a distraction. Some people like to cover themselves with clutter and keep busy with their mess to avoid their deep-down emotions. If this is where you are at, address your emotional issues first. This is scary, so seek help. Find a safe place to share and heal. Once you've healed your emotions, you'll be more focused to organize and your results will last longer.
- You want your money's worth. Owning an object is not the same as getting a return on your investment. You have to actually use it for it to be valuable to you. As you clear your clutter, take heart. The Internet and consignment shops make it easy to sell your unwanted belongings, so you can earn some money in addition to the satisfaction of clearing clutter.

Less Is More

- The less you have the more you will use what you own.
- The less you acquire the more you can pay attention to what you have.
- The less you have the more efficient you are—less time spent searching for things.
- The less you control the more you can let go.
- The less you have the more energy you will have—less energy is wasted caring for your possessions.
- The less you have the more room there is for new things to come into your life.
- The less time you spend watching TV the more time you will have to do the things that you wish you had more time for.
- The less you have the safer your home will be—too much clutter can be a fire hazard or an accident waiting to happen.

- The less you have the more time you will save cleaning.
- The less you talk the more you can listen.
- The less you have the more money you will save on storage.
- The less you have the more you can focus on your priorities and not the tasks of dealing with the junk in your life.

Get Motivated

You're about to begin a huge and probably scary task. Here are some simple ways to keep yourself going when the organizing gets tough:

- Select a reward to give yourself after you've completed your goals. Reward yourself as often as you choose. It could be for each week, each month or each six weeks you complete.
- Jump in! Once you organize one area of your life, you will realize how much better you feel and you'll want to do more.
- Ask a friend or two to organize their lives, too! You can give each other updates and help each other stay motivated. (You can even reward yourselves together by going out to dinner.)
- Listen to your favorite music while organizing.

Functions of a Room

Your home should be a refuge from a very stressful and busy world. Before you organize any room in your house, first ask yourself how you and your family use the room. What activities take place there? Don't skip the obvious—such as sleeping for a bedroom and cooking for a kitchen—but don't forget the secondary functions—such as dressing, homework or paperwork. When you know what you do in a room, you know what belongs in the room. If an object doesn't serve one of the room's

Don't believe the lie that more is better. Sometimes more is just that—more. More clutter, more to clean around, more space taken up.

functions, it is clutter and doesn't belong in the room. This will help you decide what you need to keep and what you can toss!

Don't be limited by what is currently in a room. Could you change its function to better serve the needs of your family? Would a den make more sense than a spare bedroom? Make the transformation. We all have ideas in our heads that we acquired from childhood. Many of them are based on your parents' ideas, tradition or social expectations. Don't let these notions from your past affect the layout of your home as an adult. Today there are so many unique homes and storage solutions. It's about doing what works for you. Do you really need to have china ready to seat ten guests? Does your living room really need to be formal?

When in Doubt, Throw It Out!

When you organize, remember to always start by tossing. When you get rid of what you don't want right away, you have more time to focus on what you do want. It's time to toss something if:

- You have not used it in a year or more (if it's a practical item) or you don't love it (if it's a decorative item).
- It is broken or missing parts you are not willing to replace.
- It doesn't fit.
- You don't feel comfortable in it.

Tossing simply means eliminating the object from your life. There are many ways to toss:

- Donate it to charity.
- Sell it at a consignment shop or on the Internet and make some extra money.
- Give it to a friend or family member who will use it or cherish it.
- Live green and recycle it.
- Throw it in the garbage if it is in poor shape.

When my family and I helped my grandmother sort through her

house after fifty years of living there, it was hard for her to not take all of my deceased grandfather's belongings to her new, much smaller home. As she passed on some of her possessions to our family members, she gave certain items to my husband who, like my grandfather, has spent his career in law enforcement. Since they have this in common, my husband cherishes these items. Someday, when our children are old enough, my husband will pass these items on to them.

Do you have a friend who really loves that sweater you never wear? Make her day and give it to her (trust me, if you really miss it I am sure she will let you borrow it). Do you have a child or know a younger adult who is trying to get started on her own? She could probably use that extra dish set and silverware you have stored away.

How to Donate

Donating is a great way to get rid of the clutter in your life. Your donated items should be in fair or better condition. Appliances should work. Games, toys and puzzles should have all their pieces, and clothes should be free of holes, rips and large stains. Don't waste a charity's valuable (and often limited) resources by donating items that should simply be thrown away. Also, be sure the charity accepts the item you want to donate before you drop it off.

Benefits of donating:

- You can drop your items off and leave—getting the clutter out of your house faster.
- Some charities will pick up large donations such as appliances and furniture, making it easier for you to remove it from your home.
- You can use it as a tax write-off.
- You can feel good about helping someone in need.
- For a list of local organizations in need of donations, visit www.jenniferfordberry.com/local-give/

How to Sell

There are many ways to sell your items, all of which eliminate clutter. Here are a few options along with some benefits for each:

CONSIGNMENT SHOP

You can find consignment shops to sell pretty much anything you have; clothing, toys, furniture, etc. Items must be in new, like-new or gently used condition. Many shops also ask that all clothing is brand name. Benefits:

- You will make a much higher return by consigning than you will with a yard sale. You earn roughly 60 percent of the selling price of your items.
- You don't have to spend time tagging and pricing. The shop will do it for you.
- You can sell your items and make money without sitting around a yard sale wasting a weekend.
- You have a designated period of time for your items to sell (usually ninety days or a full season), but you don't have to handle unsold items if you don't want to. You can request that the store donate the item to charity.
- You can use your earnings as store credit to purchase other things you need.
- You have no advertising fees to pay.

SEMIANNUAL CONSIGNMENT SALE

This is a new trend around the country. The sale or event lasts for about three to six days at a temporary location. You tag and price your items (usually through a computer software program) and then drop them off at the designated place of the event during a specific time. The sale owners sell for you. Again, items must be in new, like-new or gently used condition. Many of the benefits are the same as a consignment shop and also:

- You can earn a higher percentage of commissions than a consignment shop because you tag and price all of your items yourself.
- Your items will be in front of a large crowd for a short period of time so you get your money fast.
- You can collect all of your earnings in one week.

ONLINE CLASSIFIED SITES

An online "classified" website allows you to post items that you would like to sell right in your local area. Benefits:
- It is free.
- You can sell right from your own computer.
- Your items will be in front of a large number of people.
- No shipping costs; customers arrange for pickup.

ONLINE AUCTION SITES

Online auction sites let you post items for sale for a period of time, but you have to pay to list your item. You can sell to people around the country and even around the world, but you will have to pay shipping costs.

Benefits:
- You can sell right from your own computer.
- Huge audience.
- Great place to sell if you cannot sell your items locally.

Green Organizing

I am sure by now you have heard all the buzz about living green. But have you stopped to think that getting your life organized can be one thing you can do to live green? Don't you owe it to our earth to get organized? I think we all do. These small changes in your lifestyle can result in big changes in our environment:

 Reduce. Cut down on your energy usage by plugging all the

"vampire appliances" into a power strip. At night or when you are leaving home for more than a day, turn the power strip off to save energy. Research shows that 5-13 percent of a home's energy goes to these vampires. (Vampire appliances use energy by being on standby when they are turned off. Some examples include: TV, DVD player, stereo system, air conditioner.) This tip can not only help save the environment but can save you some money, too.

Reuse. When organizing a space in your life, look around at what you already have that you can use as storage. If you are organizing magazines, grab a basket rather than purchase a magazine rack. Use a cleaned-out soup can to store scissors, pens and pencils. Use a shoe box to organize and store photographs. Whenever possible use this approach to save you time and money and cut down on adding more clutter in your home.

Recycle. Much of our clutter can be recycled through donating and consigning. When you begin organizing, resist the urge to throw all of your clutter in the garbage can. Many of the items you no longer need could really benefit someone else.

Remove. Every year ninety million trees are cut down just to provide junk mail! Remove yourself from unnecessary mailing lists and make a positive change in our environment.

Rethink. Rethink how you live your life. Rethink your spending habits. When you are shopping be very consumer-conscious. Don't buy something because the packaging spoke to you. Ask yourself if this is something you will really use, or if it will end up being another piece of clutter in the future.

> *Several of the weeks in this book include tips that help the environment while helping you organize. All of these tips are indicated with this Live Green icon.*

Money-Saving Tips

Recent events in the financial world have left us all feeling a little uneasy about money. If we don't have money, we worry about how to get it. If we do have money, we worry about how to keep it or where to invest it. One way we can invest in our future (and our bottom line) is to get organized! Here are a few ways being organized can save you money:

$ **Stop buying duplicate items.** If you know that you have four pairs of gray pants, chances are you won't buy another pair. Getting organized helps you to know exactly what you already own so you don't double purchase.

$ **You will find things you didn't realize you had.** While you are going through the process of getting your space organized you will most likely come across items you didn't even know you had. Maybe it will be that piece of jewelry you thought you lost two years ago. It could even be actual money: a gift card, a savings bond or even better—cash!

$ **Get your money's worth from items.** If you own things that you do not use or enjoy, you wasted money purchasing those things. If you can't see or find an item, you probably won't use it. When you organize a space, make sure everything is visible. If you can see everything in your refrigerator, you are more likely to use the food before it spoils.

$ **Eliminate late fees.** If you are unorganized, you may be routinely paying unnecessary costs such as late fees and incurring higher interest rates because of your irregular payment history. When you organize your finances, you may also find that you've been paying for something you're not using, like a gym membership or even a storage unit rental fee.

💲 Save time. You know the saying, time is money. Gaining efficiencies through the organizing process means you are getting back some of your time. Actually, time is more precious than money, because you can never get that wasted time back. Not spending an hour a week searching for items you need means you have another hour to spend on things that are truly important to you.

💲 Sell property faster. If you want to sell your home, you can help speed up the process by decluttering the house. It is proven that potential buyers want to be able to see themselves living in your home. When your home is cluttered or full of your personal belongings it makes it harder for the buyer to see the potential. Plus closets and storage areas look bigger with fewer items in them.

💲 Tax deductions. There are items in your home that you don't use or that you don't love. If these items are in good working order, donate them to a non-profit organization. Get a receipt for your donation and deduct the cash equivalent from your income taxes.

💲 Less stress, better health. Clutter causes stress and stress harms our health. We all know health care is expensive. According to a 2003 Fast Company magazine article, the Centers for Disease Control and Prevention state unequivocally that 80 percent of our medical expenditures are now stress-related. Getting control of your belongings and your finances means you will experience less stress, which means less cost in health expenses.

💲 *Several of the weeks in this book include tips that help you save money while helping you organize. All of these tips are indicated with this Money Saving icon.*

Organize Yourself

WEEK ONE | Organize Your Mind & Life Vision

If you want to get your life organized, I firmly believe that you should start on the inside first. Why do you want to get organized? What does an organized life look like to you? How will being organized improve your life? In other words, what is your vision for your life?

Have you ever stopped to think about what your ideal vision is for your life? Your ideal life vision is a snapshot of what you would love your life to look like if you could do anything. (First, you have to believe you can accomplish anything you put your mind to.) At this particular point in your life you may feel that making a major change is too difficult, or even impossible. That's okay; you don't have to do it all right now. Once you create your vision, you can begin to take steps (even tiny steps) toward making that vision a reality.

There is a common saying: If we change our thoughts, we can change the world. I believe this to be true, and I feel fortunate that, in any given moment, I can choose to change my mind.

Your actions are influenced by your thoughts and your thoughts coincide with your feelings, so it is important to pay attention to your feelings. Your long To Do list is not what causes you stress—the way you feel about the list determines your thoughts about it. If that list makes you feel overwhelmed, then you will think you cannot possibly complete all those tasks, and those thoughts may make you feel like procrastinating or not doing it at all.

If you are having trouble putting your vision in motion, pause and ask yourself what is stopping you. You may find deeper issues that must be addressed. Don't be afraid to confront them.

THIS WEEK'S GOALS:

○ Write out your vision for your life. Answer these questions to help you find inspiration. If you could do anything...

Where would you live?

How would you earn an income?

What would your days look like?

What would you do for fun?

What would you do more of?

What would you do less of?

○ Think about what you want to accomplish within the next fifty-six weeks. When you look back on this time in your life, what will you remember? What will you be proud of? List these goals. Break big goals down into smaller pieces to make them more achievable.

○ Get a minimum of seven hours of sleep per night. If this sounds impossible, you may need to make sleep a priority in your life and readjust your schedule accordingly. What is so important that it is keeping you from getting the rest you need? You're more productive and bring more quality to tasks when you are rested. Your stress level may decrease as well as your brain and body properly rejuvenate.

○ Start your day by jotting down a short To Do list of everything you want or need to do that day. This will free up your brain from the burden of remembering.

○ Start a journal. If you don't have time to write in it every day, that's okay. Use it for the days when you need to let it all out or to record a special day or memory.

○ Limit the amount of television you watch, especially programs with negative images and messages.

○ Schedule a two-minute break two to three times a day to spend time alone and just be.

○ Practice meditating.

○ Schedule time to exercise. Go to the gym, take a bike ride, walk the dog, hike in the woods, run around the yard with the kids. Every form of movement counts (and burns calories)!

○ Schedule more "me time." Turn all the phones off and plan something you love to do just for you. Write this in your planner and let yourself have fun. Fun is a crucial part of living a balanced life and will actually improve your health and well-being.

○ Eliminate energy drainers in your life: clutter, unhealthy relationships, unfinished projects, items on your To Do list that don't need to be done until other tasks are complete.

○ Take control of your time. Set goals and then break them into achievable daily To Do's. When goals are clear, you can control your time and make space for priorities.

TIPS:

- Simplify your life and your thinking by cutting back on the amount of negative information and images you let penetrate your mind. Eliminate pessimistic news, advertising, newspapers, depressing books and violent movies.

- When an intimate moment presents itself, grab it!

- Check in with yourself before making decisions. Take a deep breath, relax and listen to your inner voice. Then, make the decision best for you. Don't feel pressure to please other people.

STAY ORGANIZED!

ONCE A MONTH

○ Schedule a day just for you. Do something that makes you happy.

○ Spend a few minutes writing in your journal.

EVERY 3-6 MONTHS

○ Spend an hour or two alone to take stock of your emotional state. How do you feel most of the time? How are your relationships? If you're happy, spend time being grateful and counting your blessings. You'll feel even happier when you're done. If you're unhappy, honestly evaluate why, then have the courage to change the situation. Remember to tackle the issue one step at a time and seek help if you need it.

ONCE A YEAR

○ On your birthday make an effort to reflect on the past year. What did you learn? How have you changed? What do you want to accomplish in the year to come? After you've reflected, honor this day you were born.

Does it ever feel like you spend all your hours and days doing but not living? With the rat race that society has us running, we can sometimes lose sight of what we are really living for.

It can be easy to lose sight of your priorities during the hustle and bustle of everyday life. That is why it is so important to add your priorities to the list of things to organize. If you take the time to organize your priorities, you will have a much greater chance of sticking to them.

If I asked you what your top ten priorities are you would most likely be able to list them. But what if I asked you: Are you living these priorities each day or even every week? If you were honest, would the answer be no? A priority isn't a priority unless you act on it. Your priorities should reflect your values, not those of your boss, your relatives, or your best friend.

THIS WEEK'S GOALS:

To help you realize what your priorities are ask yourself questions such as:

- *What do I value most?*
- *What things are the most important to me? Some examples might be: good health, a strong marriage, open communication with my children, quality time with my children, peace of mind, good friends, spiritual fulfillment, passion, travel, education, fun, a clean house, fame, status, money...*
- *Why am I here? Where am I going?*
- *What is my purpose?*

○ Make a list of your top ten priorities. If you don't select them, others will decide for you. Post this list where you will review it on a regular basis. It could be on your bedside table, on your refrigerator, in your home office, or in a journal.

Perhaps it would be a good idea, fantastic as it sounds, to muffle every telephone, stop every motor and halt activity for an hour someday to give people a chance to ponder for a few minutes on what it is all about, why they are living and what they really want.

—JAMES TRUSLOW ADAMS

○ Make a list of all of the activities you currently participate in. Compare this list to your top ten priorities. Decide on activities that can be eliminated to make time for your top ten. Focus on cutting out activities that take your time but don't bring you joy.

○ Right now, schedule time in your planner to contribute to your priorities. Appointments may include:
   - *A phone call to a friend you need to catch up with*
   - *Sit-down dinners with your family*
   - *Family movie or game night*
   - *Time to exercise*
   - *A date with your partner*
   - *Reading time for you*
   - *Time to read to your children*
   - *Craft time or time to work on a project*
   - *Organize a work space in your home office*

○ Learn to say no! Set boundaries when needed to help you stick to your top ten priorities.

○ Honor your priorities each day.

TIPS:

- Read your top ten list on a regular basis.

- Minimize time spent with negative people.

- Don't forget to pray.

- $ Make a list of things you and your family like to do that cost little or no money, and then try to do as many of these as you can each week.

- The next time you are about to spend a chunk of your time, ask yourself: Does this activity help me stick to my priorities or is it taking time away from them?

- Remember, much of what the media sells and portrays is make-believe. Don't compare your life to TV, advertisements or celebrities. Live your life the way that is best for you and your family.

- Use the ten-minute rule to help you accomplish more. The next time you find yourself with an extra ten minutes, challenge yourself to use it on a priority or a goal. You may think ten minutes does not sound like much, but when you add up a bunch of ten-minute intervals throughout a week it can make a big difference!

NOTES:

_____

_____

_____

_____

_____

_____

STAY ORGANIZED!

ONCE A MONTH

○ Go on a date with your partner.

○ Take time to call or write a friend you need to catch up with.

○ Spend the day out with your child.

○ Organize one room, drawer or closet.

EVERY 3–6 MONTHS

○ Review your list and add or subtract priorities as they change in your life.

○ Spend time with an elderly relative.

○ Do something positive for our environment.

○ Complete a long-term project that has been lingering on your To Do list for several weeks.

ONCE A YEAR

○ When you purchase your new planner for the year, schedule your priorities first.

○ Evaluate your extracurricular activities from the past year and decide if you want to continue those activities in the new year.

| Organize Your Schedule

Each day we are given the gift of time. By choosing to spend it wisely and efficiently, you will reduce stress, spend more time on the things you want to do, feel more fulfilled at the end of the day and enjoy a more balanced life. Take charge of your life by taking charge of your schedule. Only you can choose how you spend your time.

Things left undone linger in the back of your mind and constantly remembering them steals your energy. A To Do list will free you from forgetting the tasks and help you plan your time so you can complete them. It's the most effective way to organize your schedule. However, only plan for about 80 percent of your waking hours. This way you will have time for things that pop up.

THIS WEEK'S GOALS:

○ Buy one daily planner to use for both work and your personal life. Using more than one leaves room for confusion and overlapped appointments.

○ Sit down with your family and plan your week/month ahead of time so you can:
  - *Schedule babysitters*
  - *Divide errands*
  - *Plan meals*
  - *Divide chores*
  - *Plan driving arrangements for activities*

○ Gather all your To Do items from sticky notes, calendars and scraps of paper (don't forget to collect those you store in your mind!), and create a To Do list that you keep in your planner. Make this list as complete as possible.

○ Sort your To Do tasks by:

A: Tasks that need to be done this week (e.g., pay electric bill). Schedule these in your planner.

B: Tasks that need to be done this month (e.g., buy a birthday present, send a thank-you note). Schedule these in your planner.

C: Tasks that you would like to get done in the future (e.g., have lunch with a friend). List these tasks on a separate piece of paper to refer to when you have extra time.

○ Once you have your tasks sorted into categories, number the tasks in each category, in the order in which they must be accomplished. If you get all of your A (weekly) Tasks done and you have time, you can tackle a task from the B (monthly) list or even the C (future) list. If you don't get all of your A Tasks done, make those unfinished tasks top priority for the next day.

○ Schedule your dentist and doctor appointments for the next year, and veterinarian appointments if you have pets. Schedule kids' pediatric appointments and family members' dental checkups back-to-back so you can make fewer trips.

○ Place a small notebook by your bed for those nights you lie awake thinking of things you need to do. Write them down and get some sleep knowing you'll put them on your To Do list in the morning.

○ Use a page of your planner for a long-term To Do list. This could include gifts that need to be delivered, borrowed items to be returned, movies to rent, books to read, etc. When you write these things down, you free yourself from the worry of forgetting.

TIPS:

- Be realistic about what you can accomplish in one day.

- Schedule meetings with a start time and an end time so they don't drag on and waste time.

- Schedule errands based on geographical location. Don't waste time with extra driving.

- Whenever possible, schedule your appointments for first thing in the morning. The later the appointment, the better the chance you'll be delayed.

- Avoid placing overwhelming tasks on your To Do list by breaking large tasks down into smaller, easier-to-accomplish tasks. Identify the large task and then write down all the steps you need to take to complete that task. Then set a final deadline for the task and work your way toward it, accomplishing one step each day.

- Store your schedule or To Do list electronically instead of on paper. You may store it on your computer, cell phone, or personal digital assistant.

- Complete tasks. You only get points on the scoreboard when the goal is made.

- Consider your time too valuable to waste.

NOTES:

_____

_____

_____

_____

_____

ONCE A MONTH

○ Pick a C Task from your list and schedule time to complete it.

○ Schedule downtime. If you are used to being on the go every minute of your life, downtime may feel uncomfortable at first, even boring. But boredom could very well turn into peace.

○ Schedule dates with your spouse, your child, your best friend—the people most important to you.

EVERY 3–6 MONTHS

○ Re-evaluate your C Tasks and set final deadlines for items that have been left undone since the last time you evaluated the list. Break the task down into small tasks if needed.

○ Compare your To Do list to your "Priorities" list (see Week 2) and make sure your activities are honoring your priorities.

ONCE A YEAR

○ On Labor Day write down everything you wanted to do over the summer but never made time for. When you get your new planner for next year, schedule in these activities.

○ When you purchase your annual planner, choose one that you really love the look and feel of and that will accommodate your note-making style. If the planner fits your style, you'll be more likely to enjoy using it and use it consistently.

○ When you buy a new planner, transfer all birthdays and anniversaries for the year.

If you dread cleaning, think of it as a form of exercise. If you are overwhelmed by the amount of cleaning your house requires, consider hiring help. Staying on top of your cleaning is crucial to staying organized.

THIS WEEK'S GOALS:

○ Make a list of all the chores that need to be done around the house. Break them down into daily, weekly and monthly activities. Then create a chore chart and have a family meeting to delegate the jobs. Post the chart so everyone can see it on a daily basis.

○ Make a "Bare Minimum" list containing the absolute essential chores that must be completed each week. When you have a hectic week stick to this bare minimum list so your house doesn't fall into complete disarray while you deal with life. Some bare minimums may include: cleaning dishes, everyday pickup, and the minimum number of loads of laundry need to keep the family clothed.

○ Take fifteen minutes each night to straighten up the house. Make it a family chore by assigning each person a different room and list this on the chore chart.

○ Clean one room or complete one chore each day. This will save you from wasting your entire Saturday on cleaning.

○ Assign each family member his or her own towel for the entire week. This will cut down on laundry. Color-coding the towels is the easiest way to tell them apart.

○ Place a set of disposable disinfecting wipes in each bathroom. These are great for quick touch ups between thorough cleanings.

○ Save space by minimizing cleaners. Start buying one all-purpose cleaner whenever possible.

> Have a time and place for everything, and do everything in its time and place, and you will not only accomplish more, but have far more leisure than those who are always hurrying.
>
> **—TRYON EDWARDS**

TIPS:

- Carry a basket around the house while you are cleaning. If you find something that does not belong in the room you are cleaning, put it in the basket. This saves you tons of time by cutting down on trips around the house. But don't forget to empty this basket every time you clean, or it will become a clutter collector!

- Make your bed every day before you leave the house and teach your family this habit.

- A family chore chart provides consistency for the entire family. Kids know what is expected of them and they know what they can expect for their chores. Keeping shared spaces clean and organized takes a team effort. Letting children know that they are part of a team will help them feel confident.

- Clean off the kitchen counter and wash dishes or load the dishwasher as soon as dinner is finished.

- As you clean a room or area, try to work from top to bottom and then from left to right so you do not waste time back-tracking.

- Let your children choose the day of the week they want to clean their rooms.

- Do tasks in bulk. Don't get out the iron to press one or two things. Wait until you have a week's worth of items to do.

- If your house is difficult to clean, you have too much stuff!

STAY ORGANIZED!

ONCE A MONTH

If there is a particular chore that no one likes, rotate the responsibility each month.

EVERY 3–6 MONTHS

Change or launder the slipcovers on your furniture.

ONCE A YEAR

Have a family meeting to update the chore chart and redelegate the responsibilities. Increase your children's responsibilities as they age. The start of the school year is a good time to have this meeting.

Steam clean your carpets and upholstery.

Organize Your Papers

Could you easily locate your family's birth certificates if you had to? Social Security cards? Savings bonds? Personal information is something you would automatically think is stored away somewhere in your brain. But would you be able to access this information in an emergency? What if your vehicle was stolen? Would you be able to give a proper description, including the license plate number? Here are some guidelines on what to record for future reference.

THIS WEEK'S GOALS:

○ Decide where you would like to store this information. You could store it on your computer or write it down and keep it in a file or safe.

○ Label each category so it can be easily referenced. Here are some great examples of what to record for each category:

A. Health
- _ Allergies (to food, medicine, animals, etc.)
- _ Your blood pressure
- _ Health issues that run in your family
- _ Your cholesterol level
- _ Your blood type and those of your family members

B. Finances
- _ Your credit card number(s) and the phone number to call if your card is lost or stolen (do the same for debit/check cards)
- _ Your bank account numbers and the phone number to call if your checkbook is lost or stolen
- _ A budget for your income, expenses, savings and personal goals
- _ Your credit score

C. Safety

- Emergency contact numbers
- License plate number and VIN (Vehicle Identification Number)
- Flight numbers for any upcoming trips
- Current photos of every member of your family, labeled with their heights and weights
- Divorce records
- Home insurance information
- Auto insurance information
- Photocopies of your passport and the passports of your spouse and children

D. Just in Case

- Measurements and clothing sizes for you, your partner and your children

○ Purchase a fireproof safety deposit box if you don't already own one. Documents that should be stored in here may include:

- Marriage certificate
- Birth certificates
- Adoption papers
- Automobile titles
- Stocks and bonds certificates
- Wills
- Death certificates
- Household inventory list
- Valuable contracts
- Passports
- Cemetery plot deed
- Citizenship papers

TIPS:

- If you store your information on your computer, be sure to save a backup copy on a disk or jump drive. (You could store this in your fireproof box.) Make sure you completely remove the information from the hard drive if you get rid of the computer.

- There are new websites and software that can help you store and track your family's health history.

- Formulate a budget for your finances. You may want to include your spouse or children in this process, too.

NOTES:

_____

_____

_____

_____

_____

_____

_____

_____

_____

_____

_____

_____

_____

_____

_____

_____

_____

_____

_____

STAY ORGANIZED!

ONCE A MONTH

○ File away any new personal information you receive.

EVERY 3-6 MONTHS

○ Add any major new purchases to your household inventory list.

○ Review your financial budget. Consider ways you can save by cutting back on expenses.

ONCE A YEAR

○ Request a free credit report to make sure nothing unusual or unauthorized has popped up on it.

○ Take new photos of your family members for your safety folder. Be sure to note their heights and weights.

○ Update your health records after your annual physical.

Organize Your Finances

To allow more abundance into your life, you must invest in your financial health. Experts say you are actually sabotaging your financial future by not being responsible with your money now. Change your attitude about money, and you can change your future. Failing to keep your finances organized, pay your bills on time and keep track of your expenses will cost you dearly. Late charges, bad credit reports and increasing debt are just a few ways that your disorganization can cost you. Commit right now to organizing your finances and taking control.

THIS WEEK'S GOALS:

○ Gather all your bills and corresponding paperwork and decide on one place to keep all of them. Whether you are storing them in a file, a basket, or a bin, make sure you have enough room.

○ Make a list of all your income and expenses. You can use a software program like Quicken or Microsoft Excel or use old-fashioned pen and paper (and most banks now offer budget tools). The important thing is to get a clear picture of your financial situation. Remember to include the due dates next to each bill. Here are examples of expenses to track:

- *Fixed Expenses:*

Mortgage/rent	*Utilities*
Phone	*Insurance*
Taxes, loans	*Savings*

- *Controllable Expenses (You may want to track these expenses for three months to get an average.):*
  House maintenance
  Transportation: gasoline, parking, etc.

Credit cards

All food

Personal care

Entertainment

Child-rearing expenses

Charitable contributions

Habits (e.g., coffee-shop drinks, cigarettes)

○ Formulate a budget based on your income and expenses.

○ Commit right now to your future. If you are not already contributing to a savings account or investment fund, add an amount you are comfortable with to your budget today and stick with it (this may mean a few less lattes per week).

○ Ask for help if you need it. If you are not sure how to balance a checkbook, invest, or form a budget, ask for help from someone you can trust or a professional.

○ If you have not done so already, set up a college fund for your children.

○ Set up a plan for your retirement, investments, and supplemental income. Hire a financial advisor if needed.

○ Check your house for valuable items that you don't love and don't use. You can sell these items to help pay down debt.

TIPS:

- Take advantage of automatic bill payment with your bank. The creditors you owe may even offer a discount if you choose to pay with this method because they are guaranteed to get their money on time every month.

- Consider using a software program to computerize your checkbook. Choose a program that works with your bank so that deposits and withdrawals are automatically downloaded into your program. Keeping track of your finances couldn't be easier and your finances will be completely organized at tax time!

- Educating yourself about how money can work for you will make you feel powerful and, therefore, make you a magnet for more money. Research various investment and savings options.

- Your fixed expenses should be no more than 65 percent of your income.

- Pay your bills online and request that your bank does not send you paper statements. View your statements online when needed. This will reduce your paper clutter, save you time organizing, and save the trees.

- Consider purchasing life insurance for you and your spouse. The rates are lower when you are younger.

- Consolidate your phone bills and calling plans and don't purchase ringtones.

- Consider paying your mortgage bi-weekly instead of monthly to save money on interest.

- Remove your name from catalog lists to avoid in-home shopping temptations. Visit www.catalogchoice.org.

ONCE A MONTH

◯ Review your credit card statements to make sure your interest rate has not changed and that all charges are correct.

◯ Listen to a podcast about financial freedom.

◯ Skip buying that coffee, pack your lunch and put that money toward debt.

EVERY 3-6 MONTHS

◯ Review your 401(k).

◯ Re-evaluate the catalogs you receive and remove your name from those you no longer wish to receive.

◯ Organize one section of your home and look for items to sell.

ONCE A YEAR

◯ Update your budget.

◯ Schedule a time to do your taxes.

◯ Review your credit report.

NOTES:

_____

_____

_____

_____

_____

_____

Let's face it, bills are not a fun thing to talk about. In fact, I am willing to bet that most of you reading this book do not look forward to paying your bills. It is just another task, like cleaning, that never ends! Organizing an efficient system for paying your bills may not eliminate the sting of money deducted from your account, but you will save time that can be spent on more enjoyable tasks.

THIS WEEK'S GOALS:

○ Decide on a comfortable place to pay your bills. It could be a home office, but if you don't like your office area or don't want to spend time there, find a place you do like.

○ Set up this area with everything you will need to pay your bills:
- Calculator
- Envelopes and stamps
- Checkbook
- Pens
- Return address labels
- Computer

○ Gather all bills and coinciding paperwork and decide on one place to keep it (preferably where you pay your bills). Store them in a file, a basket, or a bin. Make sure you have enough room.

○ Shred any old payment books from loans you have paid off.

○ Schedule time in your planner when you will pay your bills. The best way is to pay them as soon as you get paid. That may be once a month, twice a month, or weekly. Call your creditors to see if you can change the due dates of your bill to coincide with your plan. If you cannot change the due dates, note them in your calendar and place them on your To Do list so you don't forget.

Implement an organized system for paying bills that works for you, whether it is handwritten checks, software or online bill pay.

If you are comfortable with online banking, check with your bank to see if you can pay your bills online. This is fast and easy, and you won't have to waste envelopes and stamps. When the bill comes in the mail, you can enter the amount and the date you want to pay it. This will guarantee that all of your bills are paid on time and you get them out of the way ASAP. Quicken is also a great computer software tool to use for bill paying.

Schedule time in your planner each week to pay bills and check on accounts.

Try this system: After your bills are paid, write or stamp "paid" on them and place them in a basket or folder until the end of the month. (If you really want to be detailed, you also can write the check number or "online" on the statement.) At the end of the month, place them in a file. Use dividers to mark each category (electric, phone, vehicle, mortgage, etc.). This will keep everything organized and easy to reference.

TIPS:

- Organize your bills in a large manila envelope with a small calendar in it. Each time a bill arrives in the mail, place the bill and return envelope in the envelope and mark the due date on your calendar. When the bill has been paid, cross it off the calendar. (Schedule pay days on this calendar too.)

- Fewer bills mean less time spent on bill paying, so get serious about paying off debt. Check out the "Debt Reduction Resource" on my website: www.jenniferfordberry.com

- Pay your bills on time. If you can't, write your creditor or vendor a letter describing your situation. Send them something every month, even if it is five dollars.

- Save money on stamps by paying your bills online.

- Here's a list to help you decide what financial items to keep or shred:

    ATM receipts: Put with your taxes if necessary; otherwise toss or shred.

    College savings statement: Keep the most recent.

    Credit card statements: Make sure they are correct, record expenses and only keep the most current.

    Insurance policies and bills: Only keep the most current.

    Medical bills: Keep for three years.

    Mortgage records: Keep for as long as you own the property.

    Mutual fund statements: Only keep the annual reports.

    Selling records of previously owned property: Save and file.

    Social Security statements: Only keep the annual reports.

    Student loan statements: Keep the most recent.

    Tax records: File and save for up to seven years.

- Learn to save even on the most modest salary.

STAY ORGANIZED!

ONCE A MONTH

○ File all bills and statements that you've paid. You may need to schedule this on your calendar. The longer you let it build, the less likely you are to do it.

○ Balance your checkbook.

EVERY 3–6 MONTHS

○ Replenish any office supplies you may be running out of in your bill paying area.

○ Shred and recycle any bank statements you no longer need.

ONCE A YEAR

○ Sort your bills that need to be submitted for taxes.

○ File away bills from the previous year that you need to save. Shred the rest.

○ Set goals for debts you want to pay off.

NOTES:

_____

_____

_____

_____

_____

_____

_____

| Organize Your Receipts & Taxes

Check cards offer a convenient way to pay for purchases, but the receipts don't always find their way into the checkbook ledger! Gift receipts often get lost in the shuffle. The best way to keep your receipts organized is to have a plan and a home for them.

By keeping your tax papers thoroughly organized throughout the year you will save yourself time and money when tax season rolls around. Plus, you will avoid a lot of anxiety because you will know everything you need has a home and can be easily found.

THIS WEEK'S GOALS:

○ Gather up all of your loose receipts. Sort them into piles:
  - *Check card/ATM receipts to be recorded in the checkbook ledger*
  - *Credit card receipts*
  - *Receipts already recorded/cash receipts*
  - *Tax deductible receipts*
  - *Work-related/reimbursable and rebate receipts*
  - *Gift receipts*
  - *Receipts for major purchases (e.g., appliances, furniture)*

○ Organize your tax papers by category such as:
  - *Income: pay stubs, W-2 and 1099 forms, proof of rental income, interest statements, and dividend statements*
  - *Proof of expenses: credit card statements, bank statements, receipts*
  - *Medical: look up current laws*

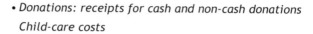
- *Donations: receipts for cash and non-cash donations Child-care costs*
- *Real estate: interest statements from mortgage, tax assessments*
- *Tax correspondences: important letters from the IRS or your state revenue service*
- *Student loans: statements of loan interest paid*
- *Miscellaneous receipts: anything that might be needed for a deduction*

○ Record the check card/ATM receipts in your checkbook ledger or digital software.

○ Take work-related receipts to work and file an expense report.

○ Put rebate receipts in your day planner and place them on your To Do list. Most rebates and reimbursements have a time limit.

○ If the gift receipt is for a gift you are giving, place the receipt in a "gifts" envelope. If it is for a gift you have received but want to return, put the receipt with the item and put the return on your To Do list. Don't put this off; many stores have a time limit for returns. If you are keeping the gift, toss the receipt. You don't need it.

○ If you are trying to create a budget or track your expenses, sort your recorded check card and cash receipts by category, then record the amounts on your computer or in a notebook. Examples could be:

- *Food/groceries*
- *Gas*
- *Clothes*
- *Entertainment*
- *Gifts*

After you record the amounts, you can toss the receipts. If you're not tracking your expenses, go ahead and toss all of these receipts.

○ Set up a small accordion file to organize the rest. Label each slot by category or by month. Categories could be:
- *Major purchases*
- *Credit card purchases*
- *Tax-deductible purchases*
- *May return (products you've purchased, but aren't sure if they will meet your needs or expectations)*

TIPS:

- Start a new habit: Clean the receipts out of your wallet or purse every week. Record any check card purchases in your checkbook ledger. Then toss or file the receipts. Place receipts that require action on your To Do list. This will probably take less than fifteen minutes. You'll also be able to find a receipt if you need it, and you won't miss out on a rebate or return.

- Keep a zippered pouch inside your purse to hold all your receipts. The pouch should be smaller than a checkbook but big enough that receipts will fit with no more than one fold.

- Don't wait until April to start searching for all of your tax receipts and information. Set up a file now for all your tax papers so you can continuously file them and keep track of them year round. A large manila envelope kept in your bill-paying area is also an easy place to store tax-related papers for the current year.

- If you use an accountant to process your taxes, call to schedule an appointment before the end of January.

ONCE A MONTH

○ Remove all receipts from your purse or wallet to sort and file.

○ Toss all ATM withdrawal and bank deposit slips after you have recorded and checked them against your monthly statement.

○ Toss all credit card receipts after you have matched them to your statement.

○ Toss receipts from small purchases after you have satisfactorily used the item.

EVERY 3–6 MONTHS

○ Toss all gift receipts from any gifts you gave more than three months ago.

ONCE A YEAR

○ Purge your everyday files of receipts from the previous tax year. Either shred these receipts or move them to long-term storage. Receipts you could purge include:
- *Monthly bank and credit card statements (after you have matched them to your year-end summary)*
- *Monthly or quarterly stock brokerage and mutual-fund statements*
- *Monthly mortgage statements*
- *Phone and utility bills if they are not used for business purposes*
- *Paycheck stubs (after you have reconciled them with your W-2 or 1099 forms)*

Organize Your Files

Paperwork is one of favorite items to organize, but I think many people would disagree. Just when you get it all organized, it seems more and more and more comes in...uninvited! The paper trail never ends, and it can be very overwhelming at times. The key to keeping your papers organized is to stay on top of them. Make sure you have a home for each and every type of paper that comes your way. Half the battle of any organizing task is to decide where to put it. So, if you have a home already decided upon, you just have to place it there.

THIS WEEK'S GOALS:

○ If you already have a filing system in place, go through your files and toss all useless or outdated information. Keep a shredder handy for personal and financial information.

○ Gather up your papers! (If you don't have a filing system in place, start with this goal.) This can be overwhelming, so go room by room, and don't avoid any stashes you've tucked out of sight. Immediately sort out the junk and toss it. Place the remaining "To File" papers in one location where you will file (such as a home office or work area). Keep in mind that 80 percent of what we file is never looked at again; therefore, chances are it can be tossed. If there is a copy of the document filed in another place or if the information can be easily retrieved from the Internet, throw it away!

○ Set up a filing system. You can use a filing cabinet if you have a lot of papers, but small filing containers (available at any office supply store or discount store) are portable options that you can hide under a desk or in a closet. You can also move them around so you can file anywhere (including in

Tidied all my papers. Tore up and ruthlessly destroyed much. This is always a great satisfaction.

—**KATHERINE MANSFIELD**

front of the television). Set up your files in a "straight tab" format, so that all the tabs are lined up one behind the other. Color code your files based on categories and do not use "miscellaneous" for a category. Here are examples of categories you may want to create:

Bank statements

Credit card statements

Pay stubs/work-related expenses

School information (one for each child)

Home and auto insurance

Health insurance

Tax information

○ Start filing! Sort through all of your "To File" papers gathered in Goal 2 and separate them by category. Use broad categories so you don't have lots of files with only one or two items each. Each pile should have its own folder.

○ When your files are set up, create a master page that lists all the files under each category. This will save time later on.

○ Choose one storage space for your addresses and business cards. Update your one storage space with all new addresses and phone numbers. If you choose to use an address book, make sure you write in pencil so you can update changes. Possibilities for storage spaces include:

- *Computer database*
- *Address book*
- *Three-ring binder with plastic sleeves*
- *Rolodex*

TIPS:

- Keep a small tray on your desk for the files you are currently working on or keep them in the front of your top filing drawer.

- If the information can be found on the Internet, toss the paper!

- The key to organizing addresses is to choose a system that will allow you to keep up with the changes.

- Use a three-ring binder with inserts to store your business cards. This allows you the space to add more over the years.

- If you create a file for a large event or activity you are planning (such as a wedding or fundraiser), remember to purge the file after the event has taken place.

- After shredding any files you no longer need, deposit them in a paper recycling bin.

- Bigger is not better when it comes to choosing a filing cabinet. A four-drawer filing cabinet houses approximately 18,000 pieces of paper. Keep it small to limit the amount of paper you file.

- Buy recycled filing products. Most stores offer recycled products alongside the non-recycled materials. As demand for the recycled products increases the price of these products will lower.

- Print on both sides of the paper whenever possible to save money, trees, and space in your filing system.

- Visit www.manualsonline.com to see if the manuals for your appliances and electronics are available in an electronic format. You can search by model name and download the manual directly to your desktop as a PDF file so you don't have to save all of those bulky paper manuals.

STAY ORGANIZED!

ONCE A MONTH

○ File the papers waiting in your "To File" bin.

○ Add any new addresses and phone numbers into your system.

EVERY 3-6 MONTHS

○ Go through your files and toss anything you don't need to keep.

ONCE A YEAR

○ Every January clean out your file folders. Make sure you have all your tax information together. Purge your files from the previous year. Only save files pertaining to tax deductions and move those files into a box in a storage area.

NOTES:

_____

_____

_____

_____

_____

_____

_____

_____

_____

_____

_____

_____

_____

| Organize Your Magazines & Newspapers

A busy schedule can make it difficult to keep up with your favorite magazines and newspapers. You may not always have time to sit down and read, so the stack of periodicals on your coffee table grows and grows without being sorted and tossed. You keep thinking I'll get to it soon, but if you let the pile get too large, the thought of catching up on all that reading seems impossible. If you truly have the time and enjoy the magazines or newspapers you subscribe to, then by all means keep them. But, if periodicals have piled up around your home because you don't have time to read them, it may be time to prioritize and pare down. Unread literature makes you feel guilty because you spent money on it so you feel that you have to read it, rather than want to read it. Here are some ideas to keep that pile from growing out of control.

THIS WEEK'S GOALS:

○ Toss or donate all magazines more than one year old. Be sure to check each room in the house for old magazines.

○ Toss all newspapers more than one month old.

○ Toss all sale flyers and catalogs that are expired or past the current season. Make it a practice to immediately toss sale flyers for stores where you never shop, and if you find something you want to purchase in a flier, clip it out and put it on your To Do list.

○ Clip what you needed from old magazines, then toss them.

○ Designate a specific home for the current issues that are left. If issues start spilling out of that home, its time to start tossing.

○ Cancel the subscriptions to magazines you never read anymore.

TIPS:

- Instead of keeping a subscription, purchase individual issues when you feel the urge and have time to read.

- If it's hard for you to find time to read your magazines, carry a current issue in your purse or car. Read it while waiting in lines or waiting for appointments. You also may want to schedule some reading time in your To Do list. It can be part of your relaxation time.

- Store current issues of magazines and newspapers on a magazine rack, shelf, crate or basket, or use a small shipping box or sturdy cereal box to store magazines or catalogs. Simply cut the top off and cut about three-fourths of the way down one side. You can even wrap theses boxes with leftover wrapping paper, scrapbook paper or a fabric.

- Use an accordion file to store articles you want to read or save. Organize by category: to read, kids, home, garden, etc. Keep this accordion file with you for those long waits at the doctor's or dentist's office or while you're getting your car's oil changed. Just be sure you will actually look at the article again after you file it.

- Don't feel guilty if you throw a magazine or newspaper away without reading it every once in a while. Tossing the periodical frees up space in your house and space in your mind—you don't have that unread magazine lying around to remind you you're not reading it.

- If you feel you do not get to read as much as you'd like, get creative. For example, read one or two newspaper articles during the commercials of your favorite TV show.

- Only read what is most valuable to you in a magazine or newspaper. Check out the table of contents so you are not wasting time flipping through the entire periodical.

- If you are saving stacks of newspapers or magazines with the intention of clipping out articles, do yourself a favor and just tear them out. You can shape up the edges later when you have the time.

- You can donate your old magazines to hospitals, doctor's offices, hair salons, nursing homes or gyms—anywhere people spend time waiting. Be sure to remove the address label before you donate the magazines.

- Reduce paper waste and save money by cutting down on your magazine and newspaper subscriptions. Consider an online subscription, read only the free articles online or visit your local library to read your favorite periodical.

- If you want to keep articles, you can do so digitally using Scanalog software (www.scanalog.com).

NOTES:

_____

_____

_____

_____

_____

_____

_____

STAY ORGANIZED!

ONCE A MONTH

○ Dispose of all items you have read or don't want to keep.

○ Clip articles or advertisements you will need for later reference.

Every 3–6 Months

○ Donate all the magazines you are done with to a charity or business of your choice.

○ Toss catalogs from the previous season.

○ If you keep magazines in your bathroom, update the reading selection and toss the old issues.

Once a Year

○ Cancel subscriptions to periodicals you do not consistently read.

Remember when it was fun to open your e-mail inbox (before the viruses and the spam mail took over our world!)? It seems that no matter what virus/spam protection I use, I am still constantly bombarded with junk mail—just like the mailbox outside! Not to mention all the emails from lists I thought I wanted to be on. Think of your e-mail inbox much like you think of your "snail mail" mailbox. What would happen if you left a month's worth of mail in your mail box? It is a cluttered mess and you would run out of room. Here are some ways I deal with the overwhelming influx of e-mails.

THIS WEEK'S GOALS:

○ Go through your inbox and delete all e-mails you do not need, including those that contain attachments already saved on your hard drive. The quickest way is to search a sender and then click delete for all under that person.

○ Go through your sent box and delete all e-mails you do not need a copy of.

○ Set up folders within your inbox to organize your e-mails by category, sender, etc. This will help clean out your inbox and make it easier to locate messages. Be sure to include a "Save" file and a "Take Action" file.

○ Ask to be removed from all lists to which you do not want to belong or that send you messages you never read. Most bulk message e-mails have an "unsubscribe" option listed at the

*You get credit for what you
finish, not what you start.*

—ANONYMOUS

---

bottom of the message. Follow those instructions to remove your e-mail from the list.

○ Update your e-mail address book so that it is current.

○ Set your e-mail to the preview feature so that you won't have to open the e-mail all the way to see if you want to read it.

○ Consolidate all your personal e-mail into one account. Free web-based e-mail makes it easy to have multiple accounts, but checking them all is too time-consuming and increases the chance of missing a message.

○ Utilize the "tasks" option. Enter your To Do list here by making folders for A Tasks, B Tasks and C Tasks. Prioritize your tasks by placing the most important ones in the A folder, etc. (C tasks should consist of the tasks you hope to accomplish in the future. Concentrate first on the A's, then the B's, and so on.)

○ Review the settings on your antivirus and spam software to be sure they are adequately blocking all unwanted mail.

○ Update your daily feed setting on your Facebook page to eliminate updates about "friends" you really don't care about catching up on every day.

○ Utilize the "List" option on Facebook. Maybe you don't want your co-workers or family members to see the photos of you and your friends from Saturday night. Set up lists for: Friends, Family, Co-workers, etc., and control who sees what.

TIPS:

- Take advantage of the "block sender" and "junk e-mail list/spam" options!

- Do not use your inbox as a catch-all for messages. If you need to save a message, create a folder for it and move it from the inbox.

- Whenever you provide your e-mail address (for an online purchase, requesting more information on a product, completing a survey), look for a disclaimer that allows you to opt out of receiving promotional e-mails and further marketing contact from the website or group. This typically is a box you must check to indicate you do not wish to receive additional information. You can stop the junk e-mail before it arrives in your inbox.

- If you receive an e-mail you would like to respond to but you do not have the time, click "Reply" and then save it to your drafts folder. Then make sure you check your drafts folder often.

- $ Change your computer setting to put your computer monitor to sleep when the computer is inactive for a certain period of time. Running a screen saver could cost you an extra fifty dollars or more in electricity per year.

- Use Google Alerts to stay up-to-date on topics of interest. The program notifies you every time your key words are discussed or posted on the Internet. For example, I set up an alert to notify me every time "Jennifer Ford Berry + Organize Now" comes up. The alert is sent right to your inbox and you choose how often you want the alerts to come.

STAY ORGANIZED!

ONCE A MONTH

○ Go through e-mails and reply to old messages or delete them.

○ Clean out your drafts folder.

EVERY 3–6 MONTHS

○ Clean out your sent box.

○ Update your Google Alerts.

ONCE A YEAR

○ Look over and update your e-mail address book.

○ Purchase and register any antivirus software you use.

NOTES:

_____

_____

_____

_____

_____

_____

_____

_____

_____

_____

_____

_____

_____

| Organize Your Mail

Do you find yourself shuffling mail all around the kitchen, not knowing where to put it? Do you dread opening the mailbox for fear of more clutter you don't know what to do with? Mail is one of those inevitable pieces of clutter that will not go away. What makes it worse is that it arrives six days a week! You need a system you can stick with. Here goes...

THIS WEEK'S GOALS:

○ Sort through the mail you currently have and toss the junk.

○ Set up one basket for incoming mail to be sorted and another for outgoing mail.

○ If possible keep a recycling bin and shredder nearby.

○ Opt out of receiving Valpak coupons by visiting www.coxtarget.com/mailsuppression/s/DisplayMailSuppressionForm.

○ To stop Yellow Pages phone book delivery to your home visit www.yellowpagesgoesgreen.org.

○ Toss all old catalogs and magazines. Only keep the most current.

○ Remove your name from unwanted mailing lists by creating an account at www.dmachoice.org. (Sometimes it takes a month or two to fully process the request.)

○ Set up a basket for mail that requires an action (a bank statement to balance or an invitation to respond to) and put it on your To Do list so you don't forget.

Don't agonize. Organize.

—FLORYNCE KENNEDY

TIPS:

- Open your mail the day it arrives and immediately discard all junk mail. Also throw away flyers and advertisements that come in credit card statements and utility bills. Keep only what you need: the statement and return envelope only if you mail back your payment.

- 💲 Opening mail as soon as it arrives can save you money. How? You will know due dates for bills and avoid late fees by paying the bills on time.

- When you receive an invitation or flyer reminding you of an event, transfer the important details (time and place) to your calendar and toss the paper. If there is a map you need to keep, paperclip it to your calendar or hang it on the refrigerator.

- Store each family member's mail in a separate basket and make them go through it.

- 💲 Paying bills online is an easy way to cut down on the mail you receive. You'll also save money on postage.

- Large, metal paper clamps are great for keeping sorted mail together in piles until you can file the papers.

- Invest in a good paper shredder and keep it handy for all documents that contain confidential information. The forty dollars you are trying to save by not purchasing a shredder could cost you ten times that amount if someone gets a hold of your personal information. Your home office is a good location for the shredder.

- Find postage rates at the United States Postal Service's website, www.usps.com.

ONCE A WEEK

○ Clear your incoming mail basket.

ONCE A MONTH

○ Make sure you are addressing the mail in your "action" basket in a timely manner.

EVERY 3-6 MONTHS

○ Toss old magazines and catalogs.

○ Replenish mail supplies that are low.

ONCE A YEAR

○ Renew subscriptions to magazines you read regularly. Cancel subscriptions to publications you no longer read. Cancel catalogs from stores you haven't ordered from in more than a year.

NOTES:

_____
_____
_____
_____
_____
_____
_____
_____
_____

Organize Your Things

Organize Your Child's Toys

I believe owning too many toys is overwhelming for children. Less is more. Having fewer toys lets your children play more with the toys they do have. I am not a big fan of toy rooms, but you may have a legitimate reason for yours—your children have very tiny bedrooms, or they are too young to safely negotiate the stairs up to their second-floor bedrooms. But most of the time, people let toys take up a room that could be used by the entire family.

A month or two before Christmas, sort through the toys and pick out at least four to donate to less fortunate children. I started doing this when my daughter was one year old. Now she understands the importance of giving and gladly picks out toys to donate. Giving instead of hoarding is an essential value we can teach our children.

There are two ways to approach the goals for this week: You can gather all of the toys in your house in one room and then start organizing; or you can organize room by room and pull out the Toss and Sell/Donate items before you assemble all of the Save/Keep toys.

THIS WEEK'S GOALS:

○ Talk with your children about the importance of helping others and ask them to donate some toys to a child in need. You may even set it up as a game. For example: For every toy they donate they receive five points. When they reach fifty points they can pick a special activity for the two of you like going to a movie.

○ Sort through your child's toys. Your goal should be to reduce the number of toys your child has by 30 percent, including toys taken out for rotation. Set up five piles:

A) Toss (broken toys, puzzles with missing pieces, etc.)

B) Sell

C) Donate

D) Save to hand down to younger sibling

E) Keep

○ Thoroughly clean any toys you are planning to sell and then schedule time in your planner to sell the toys. For ideas on ways to sell them see pages 20-21.

○ Pick one location for all of the Keep toys. Organize and store items according to categories: games, books, dress-up clothes, blocks, action figures/dolls, etc. Use see-through containers or baskets so your child can locate the toys easily. Always make sure the storage area you use is within reach of the child's height.

○ Label containers or attach a snapshot of what belongs in the container so that your child will know where everything belongs.

○ Store toys that have small pieces on higher shelves so that younger children cannot reach them. Place all small toys in individualized storage containers. For example, all the Matchbox cars in a clear bin with a lid. This way the children will get out one type of toy at a time. Tell them they must put the toys they are playing with away before they get out another set of toys.

○ When your child is old enough, set guidelines for how long he or she can leave a toy away from its "home" without playing with it. If a toy is left out past your time limit, place it in a holding spot for a certain amount of days before your child can play with it again. This will teach him to pick up after himself.

TIPS:

- If you have a toy room, consider giving each child his or her own zone to help ease arguments.

- Give your child a basket or tote bag for transporting toys between rooms.

- Remember, less is more! The fewer toys your children have, the more use they will get out of them.

- Make a habit of rotating your child's toys. Each time you switch them your child will feel like she has a new toy! Most children should have only about half of their toys out at once.

- Color-code puzzle pieces. Have your child put the puzzle together and then color the back of all the pieces the same color. This way you will know what pieces go together if they get separated. Quart-size resealable plastic bags are great for storing puzzle pieces or any other set of small toys including blocks and dolls.

- Plastic scrapbook cases or clear plastic craft storage boxes work fantastically for games when the box they come in gets ruined. I find the 14" x 14" size works best. They store nicely on a shelf and have a lid that closes tight, and you can see through them! You can clip a picture of the game off the box and attach it to the new container.

- Always make sure the book shelves your children use are anchored to the wall to eliminate the risk of them falling over. Shelves mounted directly to the wall are also a great solution to storing toys.

- Over-the-door shoe organizers are great for storing small toys like trucks or doll clothes.

- Try to limit the number of stuffed animals in your home. Only keep the ones your child plays with or that have special meaning.

STAY ORGANIZED!

ONCE A WEEK

○ Give your child his tote or basket and ask him to collect all the toys that are lying around the house and place them back where they belong.

ONCE A MONTH

○ Check the toy box for broken toys and toss any you find.

EVERY 3-6 MONTHS

○ Rotate your children's toys.

○ Review your child's toys. Take stock of which ones he plays with. Trash or repair broken toys. Donate, sell or hand down the ones he has outgrown.

ONCE A YEAR

○ Go through your child's toys and ask her to choose a minimum of two she can donate to a less fortunate child. Explain the importance of doing this. Right before or after Christmas is a good time to do this activity.

| Organize Your Crafts

Crafting is a way to create something that reflects your artistic side. It should be a relaxing and enjoyable process, so, to maximize the experience, it's important to organize your supplies ahead of time. When you are organizing your supplies and craft area, be honest with yourself. Are you really going to finish these projects? Do you truly enjoy the process of making the projects, or do you just love the idea of making crafts? Do you realistically have time in your schedule to complete these projects, not just start them? Will they bring you joy or just add another item to your To Do list? If you love it, go for it. If you don't, give yourself the freedom to redirect your energy and resources into something you can be truly passionate about.

THIS WEEK'S GOALS:

○ Gather up all your craft projects and craft supplies from all over the house.

○ Sort and toss:
- Dull scissors
- Dried-up markers and paint
- Leftover fabric, paper, etc.
- Craft supplies and equipment you haven't used more than once in the last two years (you could donate or sell)
- Craft supplies you just don't like (if you don't like them you won't use them)

○ Sort the remaining supplies by category: scrapbooking, knitting, painting, card-making, stamping, etc.

○ Decide on a storage container for each of your categories. Store like items together: fabric, paintbrushes, stickers, paper. Label each container with what it contains. Storage containers are ideal for crafts because most projects consist of many loose pieces.

○ Find a home for all of your craft supplies. If possible, keep them all together in one "crafting station." If you don't have the room for a crafting station, store the supplies in the room in which you will use them.

○ Buy clear plastic storage containers or bags to hold craft projects you are currently working on; these are "in progress" containers. Store the craft and all necessary supplies in that container until you finish the project. If you like to work in different locations around the house, make sure the container is easy to carry. When the project is complete, empty out the container by returning the supplies to their permanent homes in your craft station.

NOTES:

_____
_____
_____
_____
_____
_____
_____
_____

TIPS:

- If you have an extra closet, set it up as a craft station.

- Over-the-door shoe organizers are a great way to store art supplies such as paint, brushes, crayons, clay, or even scrapbooking supplies: stickers in one, ribbon in another, glue in another, and so on.

- Purchase extra supplies for each category. For example, keep a pair of scissors with your scrapbooking supplies and another pair with your knitting supplies. That way everything you need is together in one container when you need it.

- Baby food jars are great for storing smaller items.

- Before you start a craft project, know what you are going to do with your final product. Will it be a gift or something to sell, or will you keep it for your own enjoyment? This plan serves two purposes: first, it ensures the finished projects won't become clutter with no home, and second, it may motivate you to finish the project faster and give you more satisfaction in your work.

- Limit the number of projects you start by limiting the number of "in progress" containers you allow yourself. You should only have enough containers to accommodate the number of projects you can comfortably and reasonably work on. If you can handle three different projects at once, you can have three "in progress" containers. If you can only handle one project at a time, you only need one "in progress" container.

- Nurture a child's creative spirit and let him or her have your leftover craft supplies.

ONCE A MONTH

○ Straighten up your crafts station.

EVERY 3–6 MONTHS

○ Make time in your planner to finish a project you have been working on for several months.

ONCE A YEAR

○ Either finish or let go of any craft projects you have let sit around for more than a year.

○ Throw out materials that are no longer usable, such as dried glue or markers.

NOTES:

_____

_____

_____

_____

_____

_____

_____

_____

_____

_____

_____

_____

_____

_____

| Organize Your Photographs

Photographs are proof of the lives we've lived thus far. Pictures can take us back in time to the memories we cherish. This is why it is so important to keep these photographs organized and protected. If you have not kept up with this project it will be easier to break up this project into smaller steps.

THIS WEEK'S GOALS:

○ Sort through your photographs and make three piles:
   A. Toss
   B. Give doubles to friends and family
   C. Keep

○ Sort through all keep photos and divide into piles by date or event.

○ Write the date or event on the back of each photo now, while you can remember. Start with your most recent photos and work back through the older photos. Use an old calendar to help you remember specific dates. If you have very old photos, at least try to label them with the year and season (winter, spring, summer, fall) when the photo was taken.

○ Decide how you would like to store your pictures and purchase the necessary product. Here are some great options:
   • *Scrapbooks*   • *Slip-in photo albums*
   • *Photo boxes*   • *Bulletin boards*
   • *Collages*

○ Fill your newly purchased photo albums or photo boxes. Always start with the most recent and continue from there.

○ Organize your digital photos by month or season and year. For example 2019 Fall. Download all pictures from your phone onto a computer or jump drive.

TIPS:

- If you download pictures from a digital camera or phone onto your computer, save pictures from different activities in their own folder named according to the event (e.g., Vacation 2011).

- 💲 Digital cameras/phones are a great way to save time and money. You can print only the photos you want and e-mail the images to friends and family instead of dealing with double prints.

- When you download digital pictures onto your computer, save backup copies of the files on a recordable CD or flash (jump) drive. Your pictures will be safe even if your hard drive crashes or your computer gets a virus. Label the CD with the event and keep it in a fireproof box.

- If you use a 35mm camera, develop your film as soon as the roll is finished. Don't let film sit around until you are wondering what was on the roll in the first place.

- Organize and store your photos within a week of getting them developed even if you plan to scrapbook them later. Label the photos with the date, event and names of people, and place them in a photo box. This will help you find the pictures and remember details when you finally have time to scrapbook them.

- Photo albums that allow you to slide the pictures in are much faster than using the albums with sticky pages.

- If you use photo boxes, separate events, seasons, and years with index or recipe cards.

- Plastic baseball card slips are the perfect organizer for wallet-sized pictures. You can find these at office supply stores.

- Never order double prints unless you really need them.

- When sorting through photos toss all doubles and photos that are blurry.

- Consider preserving and displaying your photos in digital scrapbooks. I heavily researched these, and when I added up the cost of developing the pictures and purchasing a photo album, I realized it cost about the same to make a personalized digital scrapbook. The best part is the digital scrapbooks take up a lot less space! My favorite site is www.mixbook.com. I love it because the site lets you add as many photos as you want to one book. The software is easy to use and when you upload pictures, you can easily post them to social media sites and photo sharing sites.

NOTES:

_____

_____

_____

_____

_____

_____

_____

_____

_____

_____

ONCE A MONTH

○ Download all the pictures on your digital camera or phone.

○ Label all photos you have printed.

○ Properly store the photos. Schedule time in your planner to work on your photo albums or scrapbooks. If you don't make this a priority it is pointless to print the pictures. They will just end up in a drawer or box and in the future nobody will be able to enjoy them.

○ Send out any doubles you have with greeting cards.

EVERY 3-6 MONTHS

○ Delete any old pictures off your digital camera and phone.

○ Schedule any appointments you need for professional photography; for example, a family photo for holiday cards or your child's school pictures.

ONCE A YEAR

○ Update the photos you have on display in frames. Be sure to properly store the old photos you remove from the frames.

○ Around December 31 or January 1 take a few minutes to look over the photos from the previous year and reminisce about the year's events.

○ Take steps to preserve any photos that may be getting damaged by time or excessive handling.

Organize Your Purse

A purse is more than just a stylish container to carry around your belongings; it is a symbol of your need to contain and organize your life. The function of your purse should be to carry what you need while on the go, and you should be able to access everything quickly. To make life easier always try to purchase bags with compartments that will keep items sorted.

THIS WEEK'S GOALS:

○ Empty your purse or wallet of all contents.

○ Sort through all receipts and throw out the ones that you no longer need.

○ Place the remaining receipts in an envelope. (See Week 8, Organize Your Receipts & Taxes.)

○ Collect all loose change and store it in a change purse or pocket. If it doesn't all fit, take some out.

○ Sort through all debit and credit cards. Cancel and shred any you no longer use.

○ Make a list of all remaining cards and include the name of the company, account number, expiration date and phone number. Keep this in a safe place at home in case your purse or wallet is ever stolen. (See Week 5, Organize Your Personal Information.)

○ Evaluate the condition of the purse or wallet you are using. If it's showing a lot of wear and tear, it may be time for a new one.

Four steps to achievement.
Plan purposefully, prepare
prayerfully, proceed posi-
tively, pursue persistently.

—**WILLIAM ARTHUR WARD**

○ Organize your purse into zones. Keep your money and credit/debit cards in one zipped pocket or wallet. Place all makeup and beauty supplies in a small bag. Place first aid items and medications in another small bag. Keep communication tools such as your cell phone and planner in another zone.

○ Papers and receipts are easy to stuff in your purse or wallet, but hard to find once they get in there. Most people actually use only about 20 percent of the items they carry with them, so limit what you bring along. If you have important papers you need to carry with you, such as the grocery list, receipts or bills to pay, keep them together with a paper clip so they are easy to locate.

○ Put a pen in your purse and always put it back in the same spot so it can be easily found when you need it.

NOTES:

TIPS:

- Simplify your purse by only keeping one debit card, one or two credit cards, your driver's license, your checkbook and some cash. The less you have in there the less you'll have to deal with if it gets stolen.

- Keep a small notebook in your purse to list items you want to buy, books you want to read, movies you want to see, restaurants you want to try, CDs you want to buy, and so on.

- If you anticipate a delay, carry something to read in your bag.

- Keep a zippered pouch in your purse for receipts. It should be smaller than a checkbook but big enough to store receipts with no more than one fold.

- If your purse hurts your shoulder or your back when you carry it, it's too heavy! Cut down on what you carry in it.

- When possible store small, loose items in the pockets of your purse. This will save you time because you won't need to dig for them later. It also keeps your purse more organized.

- Put personal items in zippered pockets on the inside of the purse so they are out of sight.

- The Key Ring Reward Cards app is great for storing reward cards so that you don't have to carry them.

NOTES:

_____

_____

_____

_____

_____

STAY ORGANIZED!

ONCE A MONTH

○ Eliminate all unnecessary papers from your purse, such as old grocery lists, errands, To Do lists and receipts.

○ At the beginning of the month empty your receipt pouch, and sort and file receipts.

EVERY 3-6 MONTHS

○ Clean out your purse or wallet and eliminate everything that does not need to be in it.

○ Take a close look at the purses you are using and evaluate if it is time to toss it and buy a new one.

ONCE A YEAR

○ Sell or donate all handbags that you know you will not use again.

Organize Your Vehicle

Let's face it, we spend a lot of time in our vehicles. Wouldn't you rather drive around in a clean, clutter-free environment than one with garbage lying on the floor, windows you can barely see out of and a nasty, lingering smell? Like our homes, our vehicles are a reflection of who we are.

THIS WEEK'S GOALS:

○ Remove all garbage and items that do not belong in your vehicle. Don't forget the trunk!

○ Take out all floor mats and shake well. Wash if nessecary.

○ Clean out the glove compartment.

○ Vacuum the interior. Dust and wipe down the dashboard, drink holders and doors, and spray fabric protector on the seats.

○ Place all CDs in a case.

○ Clean the windows.

○ Attach a trash bag to the back of one of the seats or the console and be sure your family uses it.

○ Wash the exterior.

○ Place loose items in the trunk in containers so they do not slide around as you drive.

○ Schedule an oil change or do it yourself.

○ Put together or update your emergency kit. A good kit should include a well-stocked first aid kit, road flares, a flashlight

*Just love the journey that
you're on. In all you do...*

—SARA EVANS

with extra batteries and everything needed to change a flat tire.

○ Collect all information pertaining to vehicle repairs and maintenance and keep it in one location, such as the glove box or a file in your home.

○ Keep these items in your vehicle:
- _ Sunglasses
- _ Valid insurance certificate
- _ Vehicle registration
- _ Car manual
- _ Pen and paper
- _ Local map
- _ Napkins/tissues
- _ Flashlight
- _ Hands-free earpiece for cell phone
- _ Car charger for cell phone
- _ Snow scraper/brush
- _ Umbrella

○ Keep these items in the trunk:
- _ Can of oil
- _ Windshield washer fluid
- _ Spare tire
- _ Jack/lug wrench
- _ Air compressor with adapter for cigarette lighter
- _ Jumper cables

TIPS:

- When you visit a drive-thru restaurant, place all used napkins and wrappers back in the bag the food came in instead of on the floor. Take the bag with you when you get out of the car so you are sure to throw it away.

- Store emergency items under the seats or in the back of your vehicle.

- Whenever possible, store items in the trunk in basket or container.

- Keep an extra lint roller in your glove box.

- Keep a small tote of books or toys in your vehicle for those times when the kids need something to keep them occupied.

- Choose one location for your vehicle repair and maintenance. This will ensure that you are not overlapping repairs and procedures.

- 💲 If you can help it, don't store a lot of things in your trunk. Added weight lowers fuel economy.

- Use an old, plastic baby wipes box to organize a first aid kit for your vehicle.

NOTES:

_____

_____

_____

_____

_____

_____

ONCE A MONTH

○ Clean the vehicle inside and out.

EVERY 3-6 MONTHS

○ Schedule an oil change.

○ Check your tire pressure.

ONCE A YEAR

○ If your state or county requires it, send in your inspection.

○ Check the air pressure in your spare tire.

○ Update any insurance changes.

○ Check and change your antifreeze in the fall.

○ Update your emergency kit for the colder months. If you live in an area with snow and ice, you may want to keep a snow shovel, kitty litter or sand (for traction), and a blanket in your trunk during the winter.

○ Wax your vehicle.

| Organize Your Pet

Since writing the first edition of Organize Now!, my family has had to deal with our dog Reece being diagnosed with a harming disease and eventually putting him to rest. We've since welcomed a new puppy into our family. Both of these experiences taught me many lessons and a few more organizing tips.

Pets are like children—we need to care for them and we need to organize for them. Also like children, they can have a lot of stuff and we must designate a home for their belongings so they are easily located. Whether you store your pet supplies in your garage, a corner of your mudroom, a cabinet in your kitchen or a basket near the back door, choose a place that is convenient and has enough room to organize everything your pet needs in one place.

THIS WEEK'S GOALS:

○ Choose a convenient place to store and organize all of your pet supplies.

○ Gather up all of your pet's accessories—bowls, leashes, brushes, medicines—and organize them in the newly designated pet area. A basket for toys works great if you want your pet to have access to the toys when it feels like playing.

○ Toss:
- *Old, rusty or broken cages*
- *Toys your pet won't play with or are too disgusting to keep around*
- *All the items leftover from a deceased pet that you no longer need*

*The greatness of a nation
and its moral progress can
be judged by the way its
animals are treated.*

—MAHATMA GANDHI

- *Rusty leashes*
- *Treats your pet refuses to eat*

○ Wash all bowls and water dispensers.

○ Bathe your pet and clean its collar.

○ Check the condition of your pet's sleeping area. If you have a dog and it has a bed, wash it; or, if it's in terrible shape, toss it and buy a new one.

○ If you have a cat, empty all litter from its box, scrub it clean and refill with fresh litter. Evaluate the location of the litter box. It should be in a very low traffic area, and there should be room to store fresh litter, a scoop and a trash can so cleanup is easy.

○ If you have a caged animal such as a bird or hamster, clean the cage and evaluate its location. Does it get enough attention where it is? If the animal is active at night, does it disturb family members' sleep where it is?

○ Organize pet health records of checkups, vaccinations, major illnesses, surgeries, medical tests and treatments, licenses and prescriptions. Dedicate a file for each pet or for all of your pets in general if the information will fit. It is important to have all of this information in one place so that if an emergency happens it is easy to locate.

○ Keep a complete pet description, license number, feeding directions and names of veterinarians. Print out a pet health record for traveling, for changing vets or for the pet sitter.

○ Take your pet to a veterinarian for a checkup.

○ Before adding a new pet to your family, be sure to pet proof your home. Make sure hazardous materials and electrical cords are out of reach; secure outside gates, etc.

TIPS:

- If your pet is on flea and tick medication, write down on the calendar the date the medication will run out when you start a new pack.

- Coat your pet's food dish with a non-flavored, nonstick cooking spray to eliminate leftover food getting caked onto the bowl.

- Place extra collars and leashes on hooks near the door or inside the wall of an entry-area closet.

- Consider a self-filling feeding dish. Simply fill the container with food and the container will refill the feed bowl as needed. Your pet will usually have to poke his head into a doorway to eat. The best part is the pet cannot dump the feeder over (a feature very useful for puppy owners). It also keeps the food fresh because it's in a sealed container. Plus it saves you time from having to constantly refill the bowl. Many of these food organizers also include a water dispenser.

- Don't forget to capture the moments of your pet's life. When our twelve-year-old dog, Reece, passed away I was so glad I had many photos of his life. I used them to make a video that my kids can watch whenever they miss him.

- Make it a priority to properly socialize a new puppy.

- If you plan to fly with your pet, be sure to have the pet's health certificate and proof of vaccinations with you.

STAY ORGANIZED!

ONCE A MONTH

○ Bathe your pet and clean its sleeping area.

○ Completely empty your cat's litter box and refill it with fresh litter.

○ Clean your fish tank.

EVERY 3-6 MONTHS

○ Thoroughly wash all bowls and water dispensers.

○ Apply flea medication.

○ Make sure nails are clipped back, if needed.

ONCE A YEAR

○ Schedule a checkup with the vet.

○ Update any changes of address on your pet's registration and tags.

Organize Your Books, CDs & DVDs

A large collection of books, CDs, and DVDs can be visually disturbing and overwhelming. Be honest with yourself before you start this project. Are you really going to use the items you are keeping? Would it be better to download the music and movies? Keeping these items organized is much more efficient when you stick with a consistent system and use attractive storage. Whether you like to keep your books, CDs, and DVDs lined up vertically or piled on top of each other, be consistent with your system. Keep all spines and titles facing out for easy reference.

THIS WEEK'S GOALS:

○ Gather all of your books, CDs, and DVDs from around your house and your vehicle.

○ Check to make sure each case contains the correct CD or DVD. Put back any loose discs that are lying around.

○ Sort through your books, CDs, and DVDs and make four piles:
- *Toss*
- *Sell/donate*
- *Keep*
- *Borrowed from someone else*

○ Throw away the Toss pile and make arrangements to donate or sell the items in that pile. Schedule times to return borrowed items.

○ Divide the Keep books by size (shortest to tallest) and then category. Clean off your bookshelves and place the Keep books back on the shelves by size and category.

○ Be honest about your CDs. Only keep the ones you are actually listening to. Consider downloading the music you like and eliminating the CDs. Sort your Keep CDs alphabetically by artist. Place your CDs back into storage by artist with the side facing out. Even though you may use your CDs in different rooms of your house, try to have one location where all CD cases are kept. It's easier to keep track of the discs this way.

○ Alphabetize your DVDs by title and place them back into storage with the title facing out. As with the CDs, have one location where all DVDs are kept.

TIPS:

- Develop the habit of putting away CDs and DVDs as soon as you are finished using them.

- Store your CDs in fabric binders filled with loose-leaf sleeves. You can store at least four CDs and their notes on each page.

- Avoid CD towers. They make it very difficult to add new CDs to your alphabetized collection.

- If you listen to CDs frequently, consider purchasing an MP3 player. You can place the contents of all of your CDs in one portable device and pack your discs away in a closet or sell them.

- On my computer, I keep a list of books that I have read including the title, the author, the date finished and a 1-5 ranking. It's handy for online shopping because I can see which authors I enjoyed. It also helps me remember what books I have already read.

- If you have items you are getting rid of, try selling them online or trading them in for new ones at a bookstore.

- Place a return address label in your book when you let someone borrow it.

- When you give a book as a gift, write a short note inside the cover.

- Toss all old almanacs because information is no longer current. This information also can easily be found on the Internet.

$ Record due dates in your planner for all library books you borrow to avoid paying late fees.

$ If you rent movies, write down the return date on your calendar to avoid paying late fees.

Organize Your High-Traffic Areas

Organize Your Entryway or Mudroom

This entrance to your home is a crucial area to organize. I am not talking about a formal entryway with a chandelier and a single table holding a vase of fresh flowers. I am talking about the "real" entrance to your home. You know, the one where the shoes pile up and your kids toss their school supplies (yep, that one—you may call it a mudroom). Lots of clutter can be dropped off on your way in and out, and guests often see this area when they visit, so it's important to keep things tidy. When choosing storage for your entryway try to find pieces that can close.

You may have a coat closet in this area or near it. Is that closet serving its true function (holding coats for your family and your guests), or is it a dumping ground for items you don't know what to do with? If so, you'll need to make some decisions about items in that closet and find homes for them. Don't worry, you'll find help here.

THIS WEEK'S GOALS:

○ Gather up everything that does not belong in this area and sort the items by family member. Make the family member responsible for removing the objects and putting them in the proper place. If someone refuses to put his or her things away, put the items in a holding place and keep them until the family member agrees to follow the rules.

○ Wash the throw rugs or replace them if they are too far gone.

○ Place a wicker basket next to the door to collect shoes.

*Do what you can, with
what you have, where
you are.*

—THEODORE ROOSEVELT

○ Sort the non-clothing items in your hall closet. As you sort, decide if this closet is the best home for each item. Can you move folding chairs and tables to the basement? Board games to the family room or toy area? Cleaning supplies to another closet or cupboard? Remove everything that does not belong in this closet and put it where it belongs—where it will be most used and easily accessed. If there are items that you don't use, sell, donate or toss them.

○ Now sort the clothing items in your hall closet. Remove all coats, shoes and hats that you and your family members no longer wear. Donate or sell these items. If the closet is still too full, you need find new homes for items, put things that are not currently in season somewhere else.

○ Install hooks or cubbies for each family member's coats, backpacks, and bags, and teach them to hang up their belongings in their personal spot when they come in the door. Label the areas with each family member's name if necessary.

○ If you have room, set up your Launch Pad (see Week 53) here so that everything you need when you walk out the door has a spot.

○ Provide a place for family members and guests to sit down when putting on their shoes. The best option would be a bench that also provides storage, such as a bench with baskets underneath.

○ Stand in the middle of your mudroom and look around to see if every bit of wall space is being used efficiently. Do you have avaiable wall space to add hooks? Could you fit in a storage unit to house school supplies, shoes, and coats?

○ Decorate with something personal that makes your family smile each day when they arrive home.

TIPS:

- If your hall closet is so full you have trouble putting your coats away, you have too much in it and need to cut down. Try storing out-of-season coats and jackets in a storage bin or another closet if you have the room.

- Keep a shelf clear in the hall closet for gifts you are giving or items that need to be returned.

- In the summer keep a large tote near the door filled with sunscreen, beach towels, bug repellent, hats and swimming gear.

- Add storage for umbrellas so that wet umbrellas are not dragged through the house. Decorative pails are a great solution.

- Use those corners! Corners are the most under used areas in a room.

- Attach clothespins to a hanger to hang mittens and gloves to dry.

- $ Instead of buying expensive lockers for your mudroom make them yourself! Each one should be about 16 inches (41cm) deep, 6 feet (2m) tall and 2 feet (61cm) wide.

STAY ORGANIZED!

ONCE A MONTH

○ Clean the windows on the entryway door.

○ Empty out the shoe basket. Make each family member put away his or her own shoes. Shake out the loose dirt.

○ Toss shoes that are in really bad shape or no longer fit.

EVERY 3-6 MONTHS

○ Empty your Toss/Donate box.

○ Switch out seasonal items such as boots for flip flops and gloves and scarves for a summer tote.

ONCE A YEAR

○ Sort the coats in your hall closet. Donate any coats that no longer fit or have been replaced by a new coat. Do the same with hats and scarves. Toss gloves that are missing a mate or have holes.

NOTES:

_____

_____

_____

_____

_____

_____

_____

_____

Organize Your Living Room or Family Room

Your living room should be a place where you can relax, read, watch TV or spend time with family and friends. It is very important that everything has a designated home so that cleanup is quick and easy and you can be ready for company in fifteen minutes or less.

THIS WEEK'S GOALS:

○ Decide the functions of your living room. This isn't complicated; simply list all the things you do in this room. Possible functions include: a gathering place, a play area for children, a work area for you, a place to watch television or read, a place to exercise. There are no wrong answers. It's your house; use it in a way that best suits your lifestyle.

○ Remove everything that does not serve the functions of the living room. Return these items to their rightful places or find new homes for them. Start by placing them in the appropriate room. You can find the right storage spot after you've finished organizing the living room. Don't get too distracted from the task at hand.

○ Break the room down into zones based on the function of the room. These zones will become "homes" for the things you use in the room. So, toys and games go in one area, books go in another, movies go in another, work goes in another. Each zone should have its own shelving or furniture with built-in storage.

○ Purge and organize the "hidden" storage areas such as drawers or cabinets. Clutter accumulates in these areas because of the "out of sight, out of mind" theory. Only use these storage spaces to store items actually used in the room.

○ Clear off the coffee table and end tables. Do not leave more than a few books or magazines, coasters and maybe a decoration on the tables.

○ Designate one spot for the TV remote control so you can always find it. You could use a basket, a drawer, or a pocket organizer that can hang over the arm of the sofa.

○ Hang your photographs on the wall instead of taking up space on end tables and entertainment centers. (Consider forming a collage on a wall in the hall or near the staircase.)

○ Keep one basket or drawer for magazines and newspapers. Limit yourself to this space. If items overflow it's time to toss.

○ Clear off the mantel if you have one. This is probably a focal point of the room, so clean it off and only replace a few of your favorite items.

○ Toss all half-dead houseplants, old remote controls, broken CD cases, dusty fake plants and excessive knickknacks. Keep only the things you really cherish.

○ Replace dirty or nonmatching lampshades. This will improve the quality of lighting and improve the appearance of the room.

○ Unclutter your walls. Take down everything and then only put back your very favorite things.

○ Look at the placement of your furniture and consider changing it around to improve the flow of the room.

TIPS:

- Whenever possible, purchase coffee tables and end tables with storage.

- Ottomans that have built-in storage provide a place to put your feet up and hide toys, magazines, blankets, etc.

- Keep wires and cords organized by binding them together with a twist-tie.

- Keep any craft or sewing projects you are working on in a basket or storage container so that it does not make a mess in this room.

- If you are limited on space, do not use end tables unless they provide storage. If you only use it to hold a lamp, consider a floor lamp as an alternative.

- Never keep more than three items on your coffee table. Otherwise it will end up as a clutter table.

- Floor space is good! You do not need a piece of furniture on every square inch of your floor. Empty floor space actually makes a room look bigger.

- Only keep what you love or use. If you have a family heirloom or a piece of furniture that gives you negative feelings, it is okay to let it go. Your home is a place that should represent you.

NOTES:

_____

_____

_____

ONCE A MONTH

○ Vacuum the upholstery on your furniture.

○ Clear this room of any items that have been lying around but belong elsewhere.

EVERY 3–6 MONTHS

○ Throw out old magazines.

○ Clean the switch-plates, doorknobs and doorjambs.

○ Vacuum the heating and air-conditioning vents.

○ Dust the window blinds.

○ Wash overhead lighting fixtures and clean fan blades.

○ Move large pieces of furniture and vacuum or mop underneath.

ONCE A YEAR

○ Wash the insides of the windows.

○ Wash the curtains.

○ Sort through the room and eliminate any items you no longer love or use.

○ Consider rearranging the room to help reduce wear patterns in the carpet.

Organize Your Kitchen Countertops

What is the one room in your house where everyone is welcome? The kitchen! This week we are going to begin to tackle this dreaded room. This is a very important part of the house because it is probably the one room guests see the most. Many activities take place in this area, from cooking to family meetings. Therefore, it must be clean and clutter free! We'll start by organizing the most visible parts of the kitchen—the countertops, walls and floor space.

Countertops should be the home for only items used on a weekly basis for kitchen duties. That means storing the slow cooker that you use every other month in a cupboard. The main purpose of a countertop is to give you space to prepare meals, so don't use this valuable space for small appliances and other items you do not use regularly.

THIS WEEK'S GOALS:

○ Remove from the kitchen anything that is not included in baking, cooking or serving food. Shoes and coats stored in the kitchen should go in a closet or utility room. Toys and sports equipment belong in the children's rooms or garage. Place these items where they generally belong; you'll find a specific home for them later, when you tackle the week for that area. Right now your focus is on clearing the kitchen. Place seldom-used and seasonal items somewhere else.

○ Clear the counters of all appliances that are not used every day. Toss all items that are broken or will never be used. Find a home for every item that is left over.

○ Scan the walls for unnecessary decorations and clutter.

If a home doesn't make
sense, nothing does.

—HENRIETTA RIPPERGER

○ Clear the counters of all paperwork, mail, magazines, news-papers, etc. Go through and toss everything that is outdated or will never be read. (Hopefully you've already conquered this clutter in Weeks 10 and 12. If not, refer to these weeks for advice on organizing your papers after you finish organizing the kitchen.)

○ Create one small "paper/mail" center in your kitchen. Everything should fit into one basket, drawer or organizing container.

NOTES:

TIPS:

- The key to making your kitchen look clean is to keep the front two- thirds of your countertops clean and clear of clutter.

- Keep your countertops clear by putting away objects as soon as you are finished using them. Don't leave ingredients, groceries or clean (or dirty) dishes lying around. While it may take a few extra seconds to put things away, it will save you loads of time later by preventing a time-consuming mess.

- Place a bulletin board in your "paper/mail" center. This is a great way to display a family calendar of events and appointments.

- If you have room, put a child-size table in the kitchen. It will be a great place for the kids to help or watch you cook and still keep them out of your way.

- If you need a mood lift while in the kitchen, place a bluetooth speaker in this room so you can listen while you work.

NOTES:

_____
_____
_____
_____
_____
_____
_____
_____
_____
_____
_____

ONCE A MONTH

○ Clear the countertops of all items that have been lying around and belong elsewhere.

○ Wipe the microwave, backsplashes, appliances and the inside and outside of the garbage can.

EVERY 3-6 MONTHS

○ Empty crumbs from the toaster or toaster oven.

○ Scrub the dish rack and the sink with disinfectant.

○ Clean the inside of your stove.

ONCE A YEAR

○ Empty and clean the insides of the utensil drawers.

○ Scrub down the cupboard exteriors.

○ Clean the stove-hood filter.

Organize Your Kitchen Cupboards

Would you be embarrassed if a guest looked in your kitchen cupboards? Do you have a hard time locating items in your cupboards when you need them? Kitchen cupboards that are overcrowded cause a lot of frustration.

Many of the people I have worked with felt like they did not have enough cupboard space. There are so many things that need to be stored in them—or so we think. If you need more room you may need to get creative with where you store things. If you have built-in shelves, cupboards, or drawers near the kitchen you may be able to use this space for extra glassware, casserole dishes or pantr items.

Another key to having organized cupboards is to toss the things you don't use within a year's time. If you use that evergreen-shaped Jell-O mold only at Christmas time, it can be stored away with holiday decorations. Be realistic about what you really use on a regular basis and move or toss the rest. You'll be happy you did.

THIS WEEK'S GOALS:

○ Empty each cupboard and drawer. Remove items you do not need or use. Toss or donate:
- Dishes that are broken, chipped or don't match (The less you have, the less you will end up washing!)
- Extra silverware—one set of everyday silverware is plenty
- Appliances you have not used in the last year (steamers, popcorn poppers, ice cream makers, bread machines)
- Jars and containers that you do not use (again, you only need a small number of these items)

*We shape our dwellings
and afterwards our dwell-
ings shape us.*

—**WINSTON CHURCHILL**

- Extra coffee mugs and cups—only keep your favorites
- Mismatched plastic containers

○ Place these items near the stove: pots and pans, cutting boards, pot holders, herbs and spices.

○ Place these items near the dishwasher or sink: dishes, silverware, glasses and serving utensils.

○ Place these items near the refrigerator: plastic wrap, foil, wax paper, plastic bags and food storage containers.

○ Store plastic containers with the lids on or store the lids in a drawer close to the containers so they are easy to find.

○ Clean out under the sink. Place all cleaning supplies in plastic baskets with handles (this will make it easy to take them from room to room while cleaning).

○ Throw out all those plastic shopping bags you have been saving with the exception of ten. This is more than enough to keep on hand, and if you need more you know where to get them.

○ Throw out any spices more than three years old. If you can't smell them, they are no good! Store the remaining spices on a turntable or stepped organizer in a cupboard (this is also a great way to store baby food).

○ Tackle those junk drawers! Keep only the bare minimum because you know they will soon fill up again. Toss all of those little pieces you don't have a use for. Limit yourself to one junk drawer.

TIPS:

- If you lack shelving, hang up as much as you can (pots and pans, coffee mugs, a wine-glass rack under the cupboard).

- Recloseable plastic bags are great for keeping loose items such as Tupperware lids or pieces of an appliance together.

- Clear bins are ideal for storing loose items in your cupboards. They let you keep similar items together.

- Lazy Susans or turntables are a great way to maximize space in cupboards. They allow you to see what you have simply by spinning it. Nothing gets lost or forgotten in the back of the cupboard.

- Place hooks on the pantry wall or on the back of the pantry door and hang bulky utensils on them.

NOTES:

_____

_____

_____

_____

_____

_____

_____

_____

_____

_____

_____

_____

_____

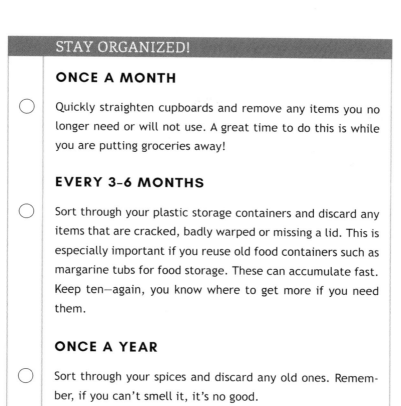

ONCE A MONTH

○ Quickly straighten cupboards and remove any items you no longer need or will not use. A great time to do this is while you are putting groceries away!

EVERY 3-6 MONTHS

○ Sort through your plastic storage containers and discard any items that are cracked, badly warped or missing a lid. This is especially important if you reuse old food containers such as margarine tubs for food storage. These can accumulate fast. Keep ten—again, you know where to get more if you need them.

ONCE A YEAR

○ Sort through your spices and discard any old ones. Remember, if you can't smell it, it's no good.

○ Empty your cupboards, wipe them down and remove items you no longer want or use.

Organize Your Pantry

Keeping your pantry organized and stocked will make meal preparation that much easier. A pantry is home to food products, but if you are like most people, you are probably storing more than just food in here. Items such as extra appliances, plastic storage containers and serving dishes often find a home in the pantry. I recently organized a pantry for a client who had a nice, tall pantry, but she was relatively short, so she was not utilizing her top three shelves. I placed items she doesn't use on a regular basis on those shelves, and after finding her a three-step ladder, she was all set. Remember, always organize to fit your needs and lifestyle.

THIS WEEK'S GOALS:

○ Your end goal for your pantry should be to make sure you can see everything in it. If you can't see it, you won't use it and you will waste money buying the same product again and again.

○ Toss all expired and unwanted items. This includes bags of chips that only have crumbs left.

○ If you have multiple containers of the same product open (chips, cereal, spices, etc.), check the containers to make sure they are still good and then combine them if possible. Then implement a one-at-a-time rule: Don't open a new container until the old one is empty or discarded.

○ Gather loose packets of food (snack bars, single-serving bags) and put them in storage containers such as a basket, stackable container or resealable plastic storage bags. Use one storage container per category.

○ Sort through the remaining items and group things by zone. The zones could be baking, snacks, lunch items, and week-night meal ingredients.

○ Organize your pantry from most-used items to least-used items. Place the least-used items in the back and the most-used items within easy reach.

○ When you unload your groceries, place the new items in the back of the shelves, behind items you already have, so you use up items before they expire.

○ Pantries are usually smaller spaces so make the most of your vertical space. If you have lots of space between shelves, buy racks that will let you use that open space.

○ If your shelves are set far enough back from the door, you can buy an over-the-door organizer to hold more food items.

○ Set up a checklist for pantry staples. This could be a comput-erized printout or a small dry erase board. Keep a list of the staples you use and put an "x" next to those you are in need of. This way the next time you head to the grocery store you will know exactly what you need. Here's an example check-list:

_ Canned vegetables	_ Condiments
_ Pasta	_ Spaghetti sauce
_ Rice	_ Cereal
_ Olive oil	_ Baking ingredients: sugar,
_ Chicken/beef broth	flour, vanilla
_ Condensed soups	_ Snacks for lunches

TIPS:

- Use the 80/20 rule when cooking: 80 percent of the ingredients are from your pantry and 20 percent are fresh fruits, vegetables, protein and herbs that you buy when you are at the grocery store.

- Stock up when items are on sale. If it is an item you use all the time, buy as many as you can. If it is an item you use only once a month or less, do not buy more than six. It will most likely go on sale again before you run out.

- Do not buy items you don't use just because they are on sale. You want your pantry to be stocked, not busting at the seams!

- Limit your family to one brand of cereal or one flavor of chips at a time. They'll be more likely to actually finish all of the product and it will get used up faster so it won't go stale.

- Step shelves will make it easier for you to see what you have. You can usually buy these at any store that carries kitchen products.

- Consider setting up one low shelf for any food that you want your kids to be able to get to by themselves, such as cereal, healthy snacks, food for school lunches, etc.

- Store bulk items or items that you rarely use on the highest shelf.

- If you have high shelves in your pantry, make the most of your space by keeping a small step stool in or near the pantry to help you access these shelves.

- 💲 You will save money if you keep everything in your pantry visible and organized according to how you shop. You will not buy duplicate items and forgotten food will not expire.

STAY ORGANIZED!

ONCE A MONTH

○ Check for open duplicate food items and combine them when possible.

○ Sort through your pantry and put items that are close to expiring in the front so that you'll be sure to use them up. Create a meal plan that uses these items.

EVERY 3-6 MONTHS

○ Evaluate all the food in your pantry. Toss expired items and move items lingering in the back to the front so they will get used up.

ONCE A YEAR

○ Empty your pantry and wipe the shelves down.

NOTES:

_____

_____

_____

_____

_____

_____

_____

_____

_____

_____

_____

_____

_____

Organize Your Refrigerator

I once read, "The refrigerator holds it all: food and finance, weight and well-being, organization and chaos, all rolled into one big cold box. Dive into that baby with a detached eye, a hardened heart and one small hour of time and you're on the road to weight loss, better household management, and a healthier budget." I couldn't agree more!

I find the best time for me to wipe down and organize my refrigerator is while I put away a fresh load of groceries. You may find it is better for you to organize the fridge before you go grocery shopping so you know what you need. Either way, keeping your refrigerator organized will not only make it easier for you and your family members to locate the food you are looking for, but it will also help maximize your food's shelf life.

THIS WEEK'S GOALS:

○ Sort and toss:
- All empty bottles and containers
- All outdated items:
  Mustard (keeps for 2 years)
  Ketchup (6 months)
  Vinegar (3½ years)
  Soy sauce (6 months)
  Olives (6 months)
  Steak sauce (3 years)
  Maple syrup (1 year)

○ Remove items from one shelf at a time and clean thoroughly. (I know this is not fun, but it is necessary.)

○ Replace items with a system:
- *Top shelf: beverages*
- *Middle shelf: unprepared foods*
- *Bottom shelf: leftovers*
- *First drawer: vegetables and fruits*
- *Second drawer: bottled water and soda cans*
- *Side door: condiments*

This makes it easy to find the food you are looking for and helps you keep track of what's in the refrigerator.

○ Replace food with the oldest food in the front and newest in the back so you use the food before it goes bad. Continue this practice each time you go to the grocery store.

○ Remove all items from the freezer and wipe it down. You may need to thaw your freezer first (summer is the best time for this).

○ Toss all items that have been in the freezer for more than ten months and toss all items you are 90 percent sure will never be eaten (let's be honest here).

○ Remove outdated and unnecessary paper and photos from the outside of your refrigerator.

○ Remove all items from the top of your refrigerator, clean it off and place a decorative basket there for any loose items that need to be stored there.

TIPS:

- Usually the refrigerator door is the warmest spot with the greatest temperature fluctuation. The bottom shelf is the coldest and has the most consistent temperature. Keep this in mind when positioning food.

- Keep a list of leftovers on the outside of your refrigerator with the date the meal was first prepared. This reminds family members of what's available so it will get eaten.

- Use one drawer in your refrigerator for bottled drinks so they are not rolling around the inside of your refrigerator.

- 💲 Before you begin a hefty clean out of your refrigerator, turn it off by unplugging it. This will save you money on your electric bill. If the refrigerator is on, it will work twice as hard while you have the door open. That can really add up.

- 💲 After you have organized your refrigerator, look in your garbage can. What is in there that went rotten or stale? This is a pretty good indication of what you waste money on. See a lot of leftovers? Consider making smaller meals so nothing is left over.

- Use the clear, plastic, handled baskets you can buy at the dollar store to contain loose items that are continuously falling out when you open the door.

- Place the healthy items that you need to eat more of in the front of the refrigerator and the fatty food in the back. This will help you eat healthier.

- Don't overwhelm the refrigerator's exterior with too many magnets. Set a reasonable limit and only keep your favorites.

ONCE A MONTH

○ Remove outdated memos and photographs from the outside of your refrigerator.

○ Check all shelves for food that's been forgotten. Toss anything that's gone bad.

EVERY 3–6 MONTHS

○ Empty and scrub down the inside of the refrigerator.

○ Check the refrigerator for "doubles" and combine. For example: two ketchup bottles half empty, two jars of pickles.

ONCE A YEAR

○ Thaw out your freezer and clean it.

○ Throw away all expired condiments.

○ Clean out and organize any extra refrigerators or freezers you have in your garage or basement.

NOTES:

_____

_____

_____

_____

_____

_____

_____

Organize Your Recipes

Sometimes it's not so much the cooking that takes time and energy—it's deciding what to make and then buying the ingredients! I admit it: I am not a Rachael Ray—I don't have all these great, healthy, quick recipes that I know by heart—and you don't have to be either. Organized recipes make meal planning (see Week 56) quicker and easier.

THIS WEEK'S GOALS:

○ Gather all the loose recipes you have lying around your house.

○ Recipes are not worth keeping unless you actually prepare the dish. Sort and toss:
  • All recipes that are ripped or hard to read. (If this dish is a favorite or you make it on a fairly regular basis, transfer it to a fresh recipe card and toss the old.)
  • All recipes you know you will never make.
  • Cookbooks you haven't used for a year.

○ There are a number of ways to store your recipes. Choose a system or product that will work best for you. Some possibilities are:
  • Recipe box
  • Three-ring binder with plastic slipcovers
  • Photo album with sticky pages
  • A blank recipe book you can write in
  • In your computer

○ Once you select your storage method, input your recipes in categories. For example:
  • *Appetizers*   • *Salads*

- *Soups*
- *Vegetables*
- *Main dishes*
- *Bread/desserts*

Once your recipes are organized, make a list of the most commonly used items. The next time you go to the grocery store, take the list along and note the aisle number for each item. When you get home, type up a list according to the aisle number and print copies. Keep a copy of the list in your coupon caddy or with your ongoing grocery list to speed up shopping.

TIPS:

- Have a collection of simple, quick recipes. Eighty percent of the ingredients in these recipes should be basic staples that you always have on hand. (These staples should be included on your pantry staples checklist from page 119.)

- Plan ahead. Before you go grocery shopping, decide what meals you want to make for the week. Use those recipes to help make your grocery list. Each night, after you clean up from dinner, decide what you will make for dinner the next day. Make sure you have all the ingredients and move any frozen items from the freezer to the refrigerator to thaw, if needed.

- Double up. The next time you have time to cook a nutritious meal, double the recipe and put half in the freezer to serve on a hectic night when you don't have time to cook.

- Do not save another recipe until you organize the ones you already have!

- Let a slow cooker do the work. Slow cookers are quick and easy to use, and they cut down on cleanup. You can buy entire cookbooks with nothing but slow cooker recipes.

- Take advantage of already-prepared items at the grocery store, such as marinated chicken and dinners in a box.

- Write or type up a separate index card for each meal you prepare for a few months. Then, when you go shopping all you have to do is pull out enough recipes for the week, and all the ingredients will be listed for you.

- Prepare lunches to go the night before. If you are making lunch for more than one person, consider using colored plastic wrap to keep them separate.

- If you would love to get your recipes organized but do not have the time, let someone else do it for you! Some professional organizers, including myself, offer this service for a fee. It's a great gift idea for an avid cook in your life.

- If you try a new recipe and don't like it (or your family doesn't like it), toss the recipe right away. You'll probably never make that dish again, so what's the point in keeping it?

- Create a favorites folder on your computer or on Pinterest for quick Internet links to good, fast recipes.

- Have a "cooking party" with your friends. Each guest should bring the ingredients for one of her favorite meals. Prepare the dishes at the party, and make enough for everyone to take some home to freeze.

- Looking for a gift for a bride-to-be? Give her copies of your favorite family recipes.

ONCE A MONTH

○ Pick out a recipe you have been saving and make the dish. There's no point in saving the recipe if you don't use it!

○ Update your staples list.

EVERY 3–6 MONTHS

○ Get together with a friend and cook several dishes. Then split them and take them home to freeze.

○ Sort and organize all the loose recipes you have lying around.

ONCE A YEAR

○ Sort through any loose recipes you've collected and throw away those you know you will never use. Organize the rest.

○ Sort through your organized recipes and toss dishes you haven't made in the past two years. Also toss recipes you made but didn't enjoy.

NOTES:

Organize Your Dining Room

As you begin to organize your dining room, it is very important to ask yourself how you really use this room. Do you dream of hosting formal dinners during the holidays, but your dining room table is a catchall for laundry, homework or projects? If you do use this room for dining, how often do you eat here—daily, weekly, holidays only?

If your children use this room as a play area, you may consider designating one corner for toys and hiding them behind a decorative screen when guests come for dinner. If you use your table for projects and homework, keep a tablecloth or padded cover on the table so the surface doesn't get scratched.

THIS WEEK'S GOALS:

Sort all of your dishware, glasses, serving platters, china and candles/candlesticks.

Toss:

- All broken dishes or glassware
- All tablecloths and linen napkins that are badly stained or dingy
- Candles too short to burn safely

Donate:

- Chipped items that can still be used
- Items that you never use
- Duplicate items that you don't need
- Extra mismatched silverware (you only need one good set)
- Extra candlesticks (only keep the ones you love)

○ Find homes for the dinner service you are keeping. Remember to keep like things together and keep frequently used items in convenient, easy-to-access places.

○ Evaluate the furniture in the room. Do you have everything needed to serve the room's function, including adequate seating and storage?

○ Remove all clutter from the walls. Only leave what you really enjoy looking at.

○ Dust lampshades and replace shades and light bulbs if necessary.

○ Take down window fixtures, clean them and put them back.

NOTES:

_____

_____

_____

_____

_____

_____

_____

_____

_____

_____

_____

TIPS:

- Organize your dining room so that it fits your lifestyle. For example, keep a tablecloth handy so you can play games or do crafts with your kids.

- Get more enjoyment from your china by displaying it on shelves or in glass hutches. If you no longer enjoy your china, get rid of it.

- Only keep what you use or love. You don't have to keep something simply because you inherited it. Give the item to another family member who appreciates it or donate it.

- Store your silver wrapped in Pacific Silvercloth, which is specially treated to prevent tarnishing in silver.

- If you have a centerpiece on your dining room table, make sure it is low enough for everyone to see over.

- When you serve meals, keep large serving plates nearby to eliminate clutter and simplify serving.

- When adding new furniture to your dining room always look for pieces that not only add your style to the room but storage as well. You can find great tables that provide drawers for storage or that can easily be converted to larger tables by adding leaves. Keep the function of the room in mind when you make your purchases.

ONCE A MONTH

◯ Clear the dining room table of any clutter that may have accumulated there. If you consistently clear projects such as crafts or paperwork from this table because this is where you work on them, set up storage bins that can be kept in the dining room to make cleanup easier and keep the table clear.

EVERY 3-6 MONTHS

◯ Take down window fixtures, clean them and put them back.

◯ Replace light bulbs for ample lighting in this room when necessary.

ONCE A YEAR

◯ Buff and polish your silver.

◯ Wipe down the walls, furniture and windows.

NOTES:

_____

_____

_____

_____

_____

_____

_____

_____

Organize Your Laundry Room

The function of the laundry room is simple: a place where you can clean and maintain your clothing. You should never store clean clothes in the laundry room. This will just make things more confusing and eventually result in more laundry. Get in the habit of removing clothes from this room as soon as they come out of the dryer. Today's washers and dryers come in all sorts of different styles and fun colors, but try to choose the one that will do the most work for you and make the most of your space. If you live in a small space, consider the new stack-able machines. They take up about half the space of the large machines.

THIS WEEK'S GOALS:

○ Start by clearing the room or area of clothes that are already clean. Clean clothes belong in a dresser or closet, not the laundry room!

○ Remove everything that doesn't belong in this area.

○ If your family deposits dirty clothes in the laundry room, make sure there is a bin to collect the clothes between loads. Instruct your family to use the bin, and, to enforce its use, only wash clothes that are placed in it.

○ Evaluate the area. Do you have shelves or cupboards near the washer to hold detergents, bleaches and fabric softeners? Is there a rack to hang clothes that wrinkle? Do you have hangers for this rack? Do you have drying racks for clothes that can't go in the dryer? Install these items if needed. Also, make sure you have room for your ironing board and iron.

*Laundry is the only thing
that should be separated
by color.*

—**ANONYMOUS**

○ Sort through your collection of laundry cleaners. Toss all empty bottles. If you have two open detergent bottles, combine their contents into one bottle. Do the same with fabric softeners, bleach and other products if possible. Then vow not to open a new bottle until you finish using the one you have now. If you buy a new product and don't like the scent or have a reaction to it, see if you can get your money back from the manufacturer, donate it to a local shelter or throw it out. Don't let unused items take up space and create clutter!

○ Toss opened detergent that is older than seven months and opened bleach older than six months. These products have reached their expiration dates.

○ Store the detergent, fabric softener, stain remover and bleach closest to the washer.

○ Give each family member his or her own laundry basket and the responsibility of folding and putting away his or her own clothes. Don't let them store clean laundry in the laundry room.

○ Teach family members to turn their clothes right side out. To enforce this, do not wash anything not in this condition.

○ Designate a laundry bag for clothes that need to be dry-cleaned. Get family members in the habit of using this, and when it is full, take it to the cleaners.

TIPS:

- Do not let the laundry get out of control! Do a little every day while you are doing something else. This way you won't have to waste an entire day over the weekend on laundry!

- Hang up clothes that wrinkle immediately after removing them from the dryer.

- Plan to do your folding while watching your favorite TV show.

- Get children involved and make a game of pairing up the socks.

- Clean out your lint trap after every load to help decrease your risk of fire.

- The plastic containers that baby wipes come in are great for storing dryer sheets. The containers will keep the scent of the sheets fresh for a longer period of time.

- Stop buying dry-clean-only clothes!

NOTES:

ONCE A MONTH

○ Drop off any dry cleaning you need done.

○ Hand wash your growing pile of delicate clothes.

○ Catch up on ironing that hasn't been done.

○ Clear out any clean clothes that have been left in the laundry room for too long. If a family member consistently neglects to put away his or her clothes, bag up the clothes and place them in a holding area. Do not return the clothes until the family member follows the rules for using the laundry room.

EVERY 3–6 MONTHS

○ Check your collection of cleaners. Toss products you don't like or don't use and combine products into one bottle when possible.

ONCE A YEAR

○ Schedule a day in your planner to take any items that are too large for your washer and dryer to the laundromat (for example, comforters, drapes, pillows).

○ Check your dryer ducts and the electric or gas hookup on your washer and dryer to make sure all components are operating safely.

Organize Your Bathroom

The bathroom is most likely the first thing you see in the morning. If you are beginning your day in a cluttered mess, you're setting the stage for a stressed-out day! The bathroom is also usually the smallest room in the house but one in which you spend a lot of time. The only items that should be stored in this room should relate to bathing, hygiene, toilette or relaxing.

THIS WEEK'S GOALS:

○ Remove everything from the countertop. Clean it, then replace only necessity items such as soap, toothbrushes, facial tissues, a candle, and toothpaste.

○ Do not let your bathroom counter be a catchall. Push yourself to keep 95 percent of your bathroom items hidden. This will not only help your bathroom look better but it will take less time to clean!

○ Find a home for everything that will no longer sit on the countertop. Try to group like things together (makeup and hair care items together; lotions, deodorants and perfumes together; soaps, shampoos and conditioners together; extra toilet paper and facial tissues together). If you have children, medicines should be stored securely away from items your children use.

○ Sort through the items under your sink, in the vanity drawers, in your medicine cabinet, on shelves, and in cupboards. Toss:
  - *All sunscreen more than two years old*

Renewal and restoration are not luxuries. They are essentials.

—CHARLES SWINDOLL

- Old, half-full tubes of toothpaste and bottles of shampoo and conditioner that you have stopped using but have not thrown away
- Expired medications
- Hair dryers, curling irons, straightening tools, etc., that you never use or are broken
- Dull tweezers
- All makeup more than a year old
- Extra applicators and old makeup sponges
- Leftover hotel samples you will never use
- Towels that are ripped or worn out

○ Wash out all cabinet shelves and drawers as you are sorting.

○ Install hooks on the back of your door for towels and bathrobes or hang extra towel bars on the wall.

○ If you do not have enough storage space under your bathroom sink, buy some organizers. There are a variety of choices on the market. My favorites are the clear, stackable drawers.

○ Consider a shower caddy that hangs from your showerhead or sticks to your shower wall to hold smaller bottles of shampoo, conditioner and shower gel.

○ If you have toys in your shower or tub, store them in a mesh holder that suctions to the shower wall. The mesh holders are best because they do not hold water that can cause the toys to mildew. You can usually find these in the baby-supply section of most stores.

TIPS:

- If you do not have enough shelf space, roll up your towels and washcloths and keep them in a pretty basket by the shower.

- Need more space under the sink? Try stackable, plastic drawers. This is an inexpensive way to gain more room.

- Keep liquid soap in a pump rather than a bar on the sink. This looks better and is less mess to clean up.

- Keep makeup in a bag instead of loose in a drawer. This will make it easier to put it away or take it with you.

- Learn to consolidate: night/day cream, hand/foot cream, face/body self-tanner, base/topcoat nail polish. Save room by using one product for both areas when possible.

- If you stop using a shampoo, conditioner, or body wash because you don't like it, throw it away before you open a new one. Don't let half-full bottles take up valuable space in the shower. Use only one at a time!

- Don't store extra, unopened products such as toilet paper, toothpaste and hairspray with products that are already opened. That way you won't be tempted to open something new before the old is finished.

- Utensil organizers are great for storing makeup in a drawer.

- Organize items based on frequency of use. The items you use most often should be in the easiest to access places.

- For a spa effect, fill a basket with your favorite lotions, soaps and candles and place it near your tub.

ONCE A MONTH

○ Replace all worn-out toothbrushes in your bathroom.

EVERY 3–6 MONTHS

○ Take down the shower curtain and launder it according to the care instructions.

○ Toss bath toys that are falling apart.

ONCE A YEAR

○ Sort through your makeup and throw away any products you haven't used in the last year.

○ Toss any worn-out bath towels or cut them into rags if you need them.

○ Empty and wipe down all cupboards and drawers.

NOTES:

_____

_____

_____

_____

_____

_____

_____

_____

_____

_____

_____

Organize Your Medicine Cabinet

Okay, this should be a quick and easy week for you. Medicine cabinets are usually small, so this won't take long. Like many areas of your home, you may be wondering: Why do I have to organize my medicine cabinet? Nobody but me sees it. There are a couple reasons to keep this important area organized. First, you'll easily be able to locate medicines and first aid items when you need them. Second, it protects the health of you and your family—expired medications can cause serious harm. And let's face it, there are those nosy guests who will take an occasional peek in there!

THIS WEEK'S GOALS:

○ Empty your medicine cabinet. Start by tossing:
- *All expired prescription and nonprescription medicines*
- *Antibiotics you no longer need*
- *Rusty or dull razors*
- *Nonprescription medicine you don't use for whatever reason (don't like taste, no longer need to use it, etc.)*

○ Place all loose items in plastic sandwich bags. Keep like items together.

○ To maximize your space, organize remaining items by height. Move shelves around if necessary.

○ Once the items are grouped by size, organize them by categories, keeping like things together whenever possible.

○ Take inventory of the medicine and supplies you have and make a note of any staples you need to purchase:

- *For pain, headaches and fever: acetaminophen, aspirin and ibuprofen*
- *For colds: decongestants and cough medicine*
- *For rashes, bug bites, poison ivy and skin problems: antihistamine cream, calamine lotion and cortisone*
- *For allergies: antihistamines and eye drops*
- *For cuts and burns: antibiotic ointment, bandages, gauze, medical tape and peroxide*
- *For digestive problems: antacids*
- *Tools: thermometer, tweezers, nail clippers, etc.*

○ Make sure all child-proof caps are secure.

○ Return your items to the medicine cabinet. Place the most frequently used items in the front.

TIPS:

- Check with your local poison control center for the safest way to dispose of expired medications.

- A magnetic strip on the inside of a medicine cabinet is a great way to store tweezers, scissors and nail clippers.

- Be sure to finish a medication or health product or throw it away before opening a new item that serves the same purpose.

- If you have a hard time remembering to take prescription medication (especially a short-term one), write a reminder on a piece of paper and tape it to your medicine cabinet. You may need to place another reminder on your refrigerator.

- When using over-the-counter medicine, read the label each time to ensure you take the correct dosage within a twenty-four hour period. If the label gets torn off, copy the directions and dosage to a blank address label and attach the label to the bottle or box.

- Keep liquid medicines in the original bottles; don't transfer to other containers. Keep pills in their original container so they are properly labeled and with their dosage instructions.

- Keep 10 percent of the cabinet empty to allow room for future purchases.

STAY ORGANIZED!

ONCE A MONTH

If you take a long-term, maintenance prescription, check your supply and get a refill if needed.

EVERY 3-6 MONTHS

Stock up on medicines and supplies for the upcoming season, such as cold medicine in the winter and allergy and bug bite medicine for summer.

ONCE A YEAR

Empty and clean your medicine cabinet. Dispose of expired or unused medications (both prescription and nonprescription).

Organize Your Personal Spaces

Organize Your Child's Clothes & Closet

Children outgrow their clothes so quickly! Keeping my children's closets up to date with clothes that fit and are in the current season is a never-ending process. I am constantly adding new and tossing old.

I personally love the double-hung rod for my children's closets. This gives them twice the space for clothes and still leaves room for shoes and other accessories.

Remember, the main function of a child's closet is to store in-season clothing and shoes that fit. Also, the more clothing the harder it will be to keep it organized.

THIS WEEK'S GOALS:

○ Toss all clothes that are ripped, badly stained and unfit to hand down, sell or donate.

○ Pull out all clothes that are too small. You may want to have your child with you to try on clothes as you do this. If a younger sibling will grow into these clothes, place them in a plastic bin in the younger child's closet, and clearly label the sizes on the outside of the box. Otherwise, place the clothes in a bin in the child's closet and add to it whenever your child outgrows something. When the bin is full, donate the clothes or sell them. Do the same with shoes.

○ Remove all out-of-season clothes and place them in bins under the child's bed or in some other storage area.

○ Empty the closet and decide what will be stored there. Do you have enough shelves, hooks and bars, and can your child reach these? Make any necessary modifications or additions.

○ Decide which clothes
will hang in the closet and which will go in the dresser. Hanging "good" clothes and using the dresser for play clothes is
an easy way to separate the two categories. Hang like items
together: skirts, shirts, pants, dresses and two-piece outfits.
Hang outfits together. This will save you time when dressing younger children and will help older children who dress
themselves.

○ When refilling the dresser, put only one type of clothes in
each drawer: pajamas, underwear/socks, pants, T-shirts and
sweatshirts. This will make it easier to put clothes away and
to find clothes when getting dressed.

○ Replace shoes so that you can see them. Try using a shoe
rack, shelves or boxes with a photo of the pair on the outside.

○ Do you need to designate a school area in the child's closet? Keep his backpack, school supplies and extracurricular
equipment in the closet only if these items are not kept in
the family Launch Pad (see Week 53).

NOTES:

_____

_____

_____

_____

_____

_____

TIPS:

- 💲 Separate your children's school clothes or "good" clothes from their play clothes and clearly label the different areas. This will help your children dress themselves when appropriate (like changing to go play outside). This will also help when another caregiver is in the home, and hopefully cut down on good clothes getting ruined and stained.

- If you want your child to hang up his or her clothes, make sure you place rods and hooks at his or her level. Make sure all racks and shelves are adjustable so they can continue to accommodate your child's clothing as she grows.

- Formula stains and breast milk can darken and become more noticeable with age, so be careful when storing outgrown infant clothing. It may be best to sell or donate these clothes while they are still in good condition instead of saving them for a few years and then finding them ruined when you take them out of storage.

- Each year I sell my kids' outgrown clothing at my annual consignment sale, Mothertime Marketplace, and put the money we earn in their college account. Check www.consignmentmommies.com to see if their is a sale like this in your area.

NOTES:

_____

_____

_____

_____

_____

ONCE A MONTH

Clean out your child's drawers and remove all clothing that no longer fits or is ripped. Keeping the drawers cleaned out will make it easier for him or her to put things away.

EVERY 3–6 MONTHS

Change your child's clothes for the new season. Get out the new season and store away the old. Sell or donate all clothing that he or she will not wear the following season if you do not want to save it for younger siblings.

Check the sizes in the hand-me-down bin and pull out any clothes the younger child can now wear.

ONCE A YEAR

Sort through your child's seasonal outerwear. Do his or her jackets, winter coat, boots, mittens and hats still fit? Donate or hand down anything that can't or won't be worn.

Organize Your Child's Memorabilia

Isn't it unbelievable how many projects and pieces of paper one child can bring home each day? My refrigerator can only display so many pieces of artwork at a time! With an end to this paper trail nowhere in sight, it becomes crucial to stay on top of this to keep things organized. I think we all feel a little bit guilty when it comes to tossing our children's artwork, but unless you are willing to pay for an off-site storage unit, there is no way we can save everything these little ones bring home. Because children never want to part with anything, I suggest tossing when they are not around, and don't feel guilty about it.

I can tell you how many clients I have worked with who saved their kids' school work, art projects and so forth only to find that when they offer it to their grown child the person doesn't want it. Be honest, do you really want all of your old papers and projects from childhood? I sure don't!

THIS WEEK'S GOALS:

○ Sort through all your child's projects and papers and toss any that you don't want or need to save.

○ Now decide what you want to do with your Save pile and act on this decision, otherwise you'll still have a pile of clutter. If you only keep your child's very best or most special creations, this shouldn't take long. If the project seems overwhelming, you probably need to toss more. The more you keep, the less you'll appreciate because there's too much to look at. Be realistic.

○ Start a memory box for your children. It can be a simple plastic bin. You can store old uniforms, pictures, ribbons and trophies in this box after the children have moved on

to a new phase. Remember,
keep only the very special items. I believe one large bin is all that we need to save per child.

○ Set up a file, a storage box, or a three-ring binder for each child's school projects. Store this in a very accessible place so you'll be sure to keep up with filing away the projects.

○ Set up a convenient, tempoary home for current year school papers Then over summer break you can sort, purge and move saved papers to a more permanent home (a bin in a storage area). You will be less attached to projects by then and be able to pair down.

○ Set up an "Important Papers" file for each child. Use it to store Social Security numbers, medical forms, school transcripts, report cards and awards won.

○ If your children are old enough, let them set up their own filing system of memorabilia and papers they want to save. Purchase colored folders to make it fun. A child who learns how to file will not be an adult drowning in a pile of paper.

TIPS:

• Pass on your child's artwork as a gift to a relative.

• Make a scrapbook or form a collage of art projects.

• Tape your child's projects to the back of his or her door, and when it gets full take a picture of the child next to the door. After the picture is shot, take all the projects down and only keep a few favorites.

- Start a journal for your children. Write down how you felt when they were born, personality traits they have as they grow, accomplishments and more. You don't have to write in this every day. Try to write one or two pages a year highlighting all of the activities the children participated in, who their friends are, and what their hobbies and interests are. The end of the school year is a good time to do this. When they're old enough, encourage the children to write in the journal themselves.

- Frame a few favorite masterpieces from your child and use them to decorate his or her bedroom or the mudroom.

- If you let your children help decide what memorabilia to keep and what to toss, you will help them learn decision-making skills and encourage them to take responsibility for their personal property.

- Remember: No time spent with your children is ever wasted.

- Digital photo books are a great way to preserve memories without taking up much space. Scan photos and artwork to add to the book. Then toss the materials you scanned and just keep the book.

- The website www.littlebirdtales.com allows children to make their own storybooks. It is a great way to use children's memorabilia such as illustrations, projects they have made, words they have written or even photographs. The best part is that they can record their voice reading the story so you can preserve the sound of their childhood voices. The books are great gift ideas for grandparent, too.

- If you can't make a decision about an item now, save it and set a future deadline (like the end of the year) to make the final decision.

ONCE A WEEK

○ File away all new school projects and memorabilia that you want to keep for your child. If he is old enough, have him do it himself to establish this habit.

EVERY 3–6 MONTHS

○ Spend a few minutes writing in your child's journal or baby book.

○ Rotate any projects you are displaying on your refrigerator with newer ones.

ONCE A YEAR

○ Sit down with your child and sort through her memorabilia in the "temporary" home. Toss projects you don't want to keep and most the rest to the "permanent" home.

NOTES:

_____

_____

_____

_____

_____

_____

_____

_____

_____

_____

_____

Organize Your Child's Bedroom

Children's rooms can be somewhat difficult to organize and even more difficult to keep that way. But it is extremely important to teach children the importance of being organized. I feel strongly that a child's room should be uncluttered and simple to maintain. Studies have shown that children who grow up in an organized home have a higher chance of completing more schooling and earning a higher salary.

THIS WEEK'S GOALS:

○ Before you begin organizing your child's room, get down to his or her level. Look at storage from the child's point of view. Are the closet rods too high for him or her? Are the dresser drawers sticky and hard to shut? Do the closet doors easily come off the track? Adult furniture and storage solutions do not always translate well to small children.

○ Simplify! Keep only the things your child uses and loves and it will be much easier for the child to keep the room organized. You cannot expect a child to keep her room organized with a surplus of outgrown clothes and toys. It's also difficult for her to manage cramped closets and drawers. The less-is-more approach applies beautifully in this situation.

○ Sort through your child's room and set up four piles:
   A) Toss (trash, broken toys, puzzles with missing pieces, broken boxes)
   B) Sell or donate
   C) Put back (items that belong in a sibling's room or another part of the house)
   D) Keep

○ Designate a "home" for the majority of the child's stuffed animals. Use plastic chains, hammocks, shelves or a toy box. Try to keep these stuffed critters to a minimum.

○ Organize and store items according to categories: games, books, dress-up clothes. Use see-through containers so your child can locate his or her toys easily. Always make sure the storage area you use is within reach for the child.

○ Label containers or attach a snapshot of what belongs in the container so that your child will know where everything belongs. Make it fun by letting your children cut out photos that represent the category.

○ If you want to limit your child's access to certain objects, store these objects on higher shelves that are out of the child's reach.

○ Clean out under the bed and place things in their proper "home."

○ Set up a file system for your child to store things such as stickers, artwork, birthday cards and colored paper.

○ Make sure your child has a bulletin board to display his or her awards and artwork he or she wants to show off.

○ Limit how long your child can leave a toy away from its "home" without playing with it. If your child leaves a toy out past your time limit, place it in a holding spot for a certain number of days before she can play with it again. This will teach her to pick up after playtime and take care of her belongings.

TIPS:

- Hang a clear plastic shoe organizer on the back of the closet door. This is a great place to store all of those little items they can't seem to part with!

- Use shelves whenever possible for storing toys and books. Shelves make these items very accessible.

- Use a point systems as an incentive for keeping the room clean. Just be sure you reward your child with actions and activities instead of toys and other objects that will clutter up the room.

- Keep a colorful hamper in the room and teach your child to place dirty laundry in it.

- Make sure to treat your rules seriously so that your child will, too.

- Before bedtime, play "what is out of its home?" with younger children. Go around the room and pick up the items that are out of place, then put them where they belong.

- Consider breaking the room up into zones such as reading, play, dressing and sleeping. Zones may make it easier for your child to clean up and keep the room organized. All books would go in the reading zone, toys in the play zone, etc.

- Make up a daily checklist for the tasks you want the child to do each day in his or her room. Post it at the child's eye level. If the child cannot read, use photos or artwork to describe the duties.

- Too much stuff and too many choices overwhelm children. Keep it simple!

STAY ORGANIZED!

ONCE A MONTH

○ Have your child check under his bed and in his closet for any misplaced toys, clothes or shoes.

EVERY 3–6 MONTHS

○ Toss any art or science projects that could go bad or attract insects, such as macaroni necklaces or leaf collections.

○ Clean out and organize the various clutter catchers in the room including toy boxes, totes and other containers. Sell or donate the items your child no longer needs.

ONCE A YEAR

○ Rearrange the furniture in the room to prevent the carpet from developing heavy wear patterns in high traffic areas and to help your child adjust to change.

○ Clean all windows and window treatments.

○ Flip the mattress.

NOTES:

_____

_____

_____

_____

_____

_____

_____

_____

Organize Your Bedroom Closet

This is the week you have either been dreading or looking forward to...the bedroom closet! Do not put it off. Now is the perfect time to get that closet in shape! The first rule of organizing any closet is to create a visible and accessible home for everything stored in the space. Always reserve the most accessible space for the items you use the most. If you share this closet with someone else, maintain separate areas for each person.

If you can't access everything in your closet with ease, you have too much stuff in the space—it is time to toss. Clothes will wrinkle if they are too close together, so don't overcrowd. Your excess clothes may be a burden to you, but they could be a blessing to someone else. I am a firm believer in passing an item on to someone who will get more use out of it than I do. There is probably a person in a local shelter who is in desperate need of a sweatshirt just like the one you hardly ever wear.

THIS WEEK'S GOALS:

○ Start by tossing! Unlike many organizers, I do not recommend pulling everything out at once. I think it is much easier to narrow down your mess first. Be honest with yourself as you go through and pull out everything you can see that:

- You have not worn in more than one year
- You do not feel good in
- Is out of style
- You just don't like
- Doesn't fit
- Is worn out, ripped or stained

If the clothes are in decent shape, donate them or consign them. Throw away any ripped or damaged clothing. Apply

*Every generation laughs at
the old fashions, but reli-
giously follows the new.*

—HENRY DAVID THOREAU

these same rules to your shoes, belts, purses and any other accessories (such as scarves or neckties).

○ Remove all of your out-of-season clothes and place them in an extra closet or in a plastic container stored under the bed.

○ Now that you've pared things down, empty the closet and lay all the clothes on the bed or floor. I know this is not going to be a pretty sight, but it is the only way you can get a fresh start. Throw away all broken or bent hangers. Once the closet is empty, evaluate the space. Do you need to hang any extra rods, add a belt-and-tie rack or put in new shelves? Make any modifications you need to improve your closet's storage functions.

○ Hang your clothing by category and then by color. For example: hang all short-sleeved shirts together by color (neutrals, pink tones, purple tones, green tones, blue tones, black). Then do the same for your long-sleeved shirts, pants, skirts and dresses. This will give your closet a more organized look and make it easier to find the right outfit for every occasion. Make sure your clothes all face the same direction on the hangers.

○ Replace shoes so that you can see them. Try using a shoe rack, shelves or boxes with a photo of the pair on the outside. An over-the-door pocket organizer hanging on the inside of your closet door also works well.

TIPS:

- If you do not have enough space, consider hanging a second rod off the first for pants. Look for a rod with two hooks that will easily hang off the top rod.

- If you need more lighting in your closet, try a battery-powered light you can mount on the wall. These are available at most home improvement stores.

- Place one or two dryer sheets in storage containers with your out-of-season clothes. This will help keep them smelling fresh.

$ If you are getting bored with your wardrobe, organize a "clothing swap" with some close friends or family members rather than going out and buying new clothes. You'll get clothes that are new to you while getting rid of old items.

- Keep a rolled up magazine in your boots to keep them standing upright.

- If you are having trouble deciding on certain items, hang their hangers backward on the rod (so the hook faces the front of the rod). If after six months the hanger is still in that position, you have your answer. You don't wear it often enough to keep it.

- If you don't feel good in a piece of clothing get rid of it. Only keep the items that make you feel your best!

- Do not keep items that you never wear only because of what they originally cost you.

STAY ORGANIZED!

ONCE A MONTH

○ Do a quick look through your closet and put fallen clothing back on hangers, and make sure hangers are facing the same direction and that all clothes are hanging straight.

EVERY 3–6 MONTHS

○ Swap the old season's clothing for the new season.

○ Sell or donate the clothing you did not wear this season—now. Be honest: if you didn't wear it this year, you won't wear it next year. Store the rest under your bed.

ONCE A YEAR

○ Repeat the entire goal process listed for this week to give your closet a thorough cleaning.

NOTES:

_____

_____

_____

_____

_____

_____

_____

_____

_____

_____

_____

Organize Your Memorabilia

Holding on to too many things from the past blocks the flow of new things into your life. According to Jungian psychoanalyst Nancy Dougherty, keeping the memory and letting go of the object is a process of growth. So, what is memorabilia? Memorabilia are all those items you keep because they remind you of a special person, activity or time in your life. They can be photos, awards, family records, letters, postcards, greeting cards, souvenirs, yearbooks and even clothes.

The trick to organizing your memorabilia is to save only what is still meaningful (keyword still), not what was meaningful in the eighth grade. Ask yourself if these items are worth saving to begin with and then only keep those that tug at your heart or capture the key moments of your life. Let's face it, we can't keep every token that we come across—that's what memories are for. Keeping too many mementos greatly increases the odds of losing the truly special items amongst the clutter.

After you have decided what to keep, the second most important task of organizing your memorabilia is to decide the best way to store and preserve these special items.

THIS WEEK'S GOALS:

Sort through your memorabilia and make three piles:

- A. Toss: This could be old appointment books, unflattering photos, letters from ex-boyfriends, postcards, every holiday card you ever received (I only save the ones with personal notes in them). Discard this pile.
- B. Keep: This could be letters containing handwriting from a deceased loved one and journals.
- C. Pass On: Anything someone else might enjoy more

than you including photos or keepsakes to be handed down to your children.

○ Distribute your "Pass On" pile. Ask the person if she would like the item and then give it to her, via mail or in person. If she doesn't want the object, you'll have to decide if you want to keep it or toss it.

○ If you are saving letters and must keep the envelope, unfold the letter and staple the envelope to the back of it. This makes it easier to see what you have.

○ Decide where and how you would like to store your memorabilia and purchase the necessary products.

○ Start putting your photographs in an album or photo box. Always start with the most recent and continue from there.

○ Consider organizing your memorabilia into life-stage categories:

Childhood: ages 0-11

Adolescence: 12-18

Early adulthood: 19-25

Prime adulthood: 26-45

Middle adulthood: 46-65

Later adulthood: 66-onward

○ Memorabilia is one of the most emotional things to organize, so give yourself time to reminisce and absorb your feelings. (Let's be honest, this could be the last time you look at this stuff!)

○ Round up your spouse's memorabilia and help him go through this process.

TIPS:

- Store memorabilia in archival-quality boxes. Cardboard boxes release gases that can destroy paper.

- If you are saving clothing (wedding gown, christening gown, letter jacket), consider having it professionally preserved at a dry cleaner. This is the safest way to guard against moths and discoloration.

- Remember to label photographs with the names of the people in the picture. Otherwise, family members who come across them in the future will not know who they are. If you can, include the date (or at least the year), location and occasion as well.

- Scrapbooking takes a lot of time, and requires a lot of storage space for the materials. If you don't make it a priority to get these projects done, then you are wasting storage space. This is why I love digital scrapbooking. I can work on photo albums for ten minutes here and there, and I don't have to pull out a bunch of supplies—just my computer! And these books are much thinner than the old fashioned scrapbooks, so they take up much less space.

- Make a baby book for each of your children to record information about their health, personality and accomplishments as they grow.

- Display photographs of family members and your heritage in your home if they bring you joy.

- To help you decide how much to keep, set a limit on the number of items you can have per category. Like everything else, the less you keep the more you will treasure and enjoy what you have.

ONCE A MONTH

◯ Toss any greeting cards you received that do not have a hand-written message on them.

◯ If you are overwhelmed by too much memorabilia, go through one bin or box per month until it is done.

EVERY 3-6 MONTHS

◯ Update your child's memory book with photos, special school assignments, award ribbons and artwork. Be realistic about what you can fit in the book. Keep only the best and most special.

ONCE A YEAR

◯ Identify new pieces of memorabilia acquired in the last year. It may have started as something practical, but if you've been holding on to it for the past year because it gives you a good feeling or holds memories, it's memorabilia. Preserve it and store properly.

NOTES:

_____

_____

_____

_____

_____

_____

_____

Organize Your Master Bedroom

We are now going to conquer the master bedroom, where we actually spend one-third of our lives! This is the one room in the house that should be your private sanctuary—a place where you can rest easily and become revived. Experts agree that consistent, sound sleep reduces anxiety and increases our life spans and our ability to manage the stress of life. Resting is much more difficult when you are surrounded by clutter, so let's get started!

THIS WEEK'S GOALS:

○ Talk with the person you share this room with about what you both want this room to look like, and then establish routines to keep it that way, such as pick up clothes off the floor before bedtime, make the bed every morning, put things away when you are done with them, etc.

○ Evaluate the contents of your bedroom. It's a place for sleeping, relaxing and dressing and should only house items related to these activities. Remove any miscellaneous items that really belong in another room, such as the ironing board (it belongs near the washer and dryer; how can you relax with a constant reminder of housework next to your bed?) and unused exercise equipment (if you haven't used it in months, either recommit or get rid of it).

○ Clean out and organize under your bed. Place all items that need to be stored here in clear plastic containers so you can easily see what you are storing. Items stored under the bed may include: out-of-season clothing, dress shoes not frequently worn, out-of-season bedding, books or movies you have no room to store elsewhere and exercise equipment that you do not have room to keep set up all the time.

○ Clear off all the junk on your bedside tables. Remove all books and magazines you are not currently reading. Books belong on the bookshelf and old magazines should be thrown away or, if you are a collector, placed with the other archived editions. If your table has drawers, use them to store amenities such as lotions and sleep masks so the top can be clutter-free, and consider storing all beauty products in your bathroom.

○ Eliminate excessive throw pillows unless they are really worth the effort of taking off and putting on the bed twice a day.

○ Clear off your dressers. Remove all but your favorite perfume or cologne and a couple pictures or decorations. Make sure you are putting your clean clothes in the dresser and not just sitting them on top of it.

○ Empty each dresser drawer one at a time. Sort and toss:
  - *Socks without a match*
  - *Worn-out underwear and bras*
  - *Clothes that are the wrong size*
  - *Bathing suits you never wear*

○ Wash and iron curtains or drapes.

○ Clean windows and mirrors.

TIPS:

- If you share your master bedroom with a spouse or significant other, remember that you need to honor and respect each other's space and things just like you honor and respect each other.

- A riser under each of your bed legs is a great way to gain extra storage space. You can easily gain an extra 4-6 inches (10-15cm), which will allow you to fit more under your bed. Risers can be found at most stores that specialize in home items.

- Bed skirts hide anything you store under your bed.

- Measure the area under your bed before you buy storage containers to ensure they will fit in the space. New space-saver bags also are great for storing items in a tight place. A cost-saving alternative is to reuse the clear zippered bags that bedspreads come in.

NOTES:

_____

_____

_____

_____

_____

_____

_____

_____

_____

_____

_____

ONCE A MONTH

○ Clear off and clean the top of your dressers and bedside tables.

○ Make sure all bedding is clean

EVERY 3–6 MONTHS

○ Wash the insides of the windows.

○ Strip the bed and flip the mattress.

○ Launder the mattress pad and dust ruffle.

○ Switch out clothes in containers under your bed for the current season.

○ Sort and organize your dresser drawers.

ONCE A YEAR

○ Clean out and organize under the bed.

○ Wash and iron the curtains.

Organize Your Jewelry Box & Accessories

We all love some great accessories—but we can't keep every one we have ever worn! This is the week to take inventory of your purses, handbags, jewelry, belts and hats. Styles and personal taste change, so the goal this week is to make sure your accessories reflect your true self: what you actually wear, what you love, what you feel good in! Remember that when you let go of those old purses and pieces of outdated costume jewelry you make room for new items to enter your life.

THIS WEEK'S GOALS:

○ Gather up your purses. How often do you change purses—every season or every outfit? Keep this in mind when you are sorting. Sort and toss:
- Handbags you haven't carried in the past year
- Purses with broken zippers or straps
- Purses that are worn or dingy, and look shabby
- Purses completely out of style

○ Decide how you will store your purses. They may be stored on hooks in your closet or, if you are limited on wall space, in clear plastic containers on a shelf where they can be seen without pulling each one out.

○ Gather up your belts. Sort and toss:
- Belts you haven't worn in the past year
- Belts that are broken, worn out or shabby
- Belts that do not fit

○ Gather up your hats. Sort and toss:
- Hats you know you will never wear

*It is health that is real
wealth and not pieces of
gold and silver.*

—MAHATMA GANDHI

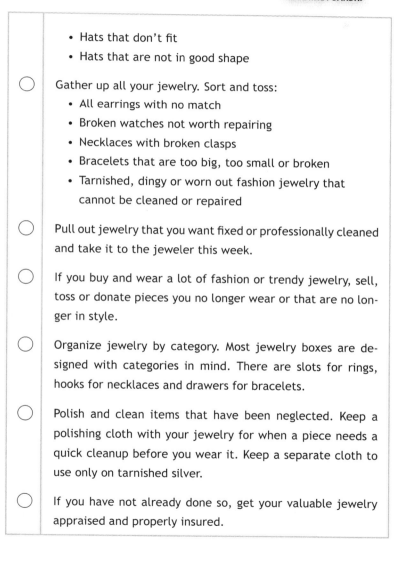

- Hats that don't fit
- Hats that are not in good shape

○ Gather up all your jewelry. Sort and toss:
  - All earrings with no match
  - Broken watches not worth repairing
  - Necklaces with broken clasps
  - Bracelets that are too big, too small or broken
  - Tarnished, dingy or worn out fashion jewelry that cannot be cleaned or repaired

○ Pull out jewelry that you want fixed or professionally cleaned and take it to the jeweler this week.

○ If you buy and wear a lot of fashion or trendy jewelry, sell, toss or donate pieces you no longer wear or that are no longer in style.

○ Organize jewelry by category. Most jewelry boxes are designed with categories in mind. There are slots for rings, hooks for necklaces and drawers for bracelets.

○ Polish and clean items that have been neglected. Keep a polishing cloth with your jewelry for when a piece needs a quick cleanup before you wear it. Keep a separate cloth to use only on tarnished silver.

○ If you have not already done so, get your valuable jewelry appraised and properly insured.

TIPS:

- Leave your best jewelry at home when you travel. Place longer chains unhooked in a drinking straw when you travel to avoid a tangled mess.

- When you change purses, evaluate whether you will carry the old purse again. If the answer is no, sell, donate or trash the purse.

- Hang belts by slipping their buckles over the hook of a clothes hanger.

- Clear, plastic bead organizers are a great way to store small pieces of jewelry such as earrings. Find them wherever crafts are sold.

- Mug trees that hold coffee mugs are a great way to store your bulky bracelets or chunky necklaces.

STAY ORGANIZED!

ONCE A MONTH

○ Clear out the purse you have been carrying.

EVERY 3–6 MONTHS

○ Polish and clean your frequently worn fine jewelry or take it to a jeweler for a professional cleaning.

ONCE A YEAR

○ Purge your fashion jewelry. Toss anything that's worn out, broken or no longer worn.

○ Purge your purse collection. Toss any purses you did not carry in the past year.

Organize Your Storage Areas

Organize Your Home Office

I cannot focus on my work when my desk is messy. When papers and projects are thrown all over, all I can see is the mess! I also know that I am much more efficient if I work on one project at a time. With two different businesses to run, it takes organization just to keep projects separated and running smoothly.

If you are setting up a home office, consider other family members who will be using this space, too. You may file papers, pay bills and balance your checkbook in this area, while your children may use the space to do their homework or play computer games. Choose an adjustable chair to accommodate all family members' heights. One of the biggest culprits of clutter in the office is paper! Keep in mind that only 20 percent of the papers we keep are ever looked at again.

THIS WEEK'S GOALS:

○ Make sure you have a large wastepaper basket beside your desk (you are going to need it). You may also want to purchase a paper shredder if you don't already have one.

○ Throw out all pens, markers and highlighters that do not work and sharpen your pencils.

○ Gather all the paper clips, rubber bands, staples, and erasers and store them in a drawer organizer. This is a must!

 Recycle everything that is outdated, such as letterhead, business cards, pamphlets, and envelopes.

○ Remove all personal items such as picture frames from the top of your desk. Hang them on the wall or bulletin board to free up space.

○ Now clear off everything that is left on your desk and clean and polish it. (It may be the first time you've seen your desk this clean since you purchased it!) You'll deal with any paper clutter in a later goal.

○ Place your phone, printer, computer, and fax machine within easy reach of your chair.

○ Rearrange furniture to boost efficiency. Bring filing cabinets, frequently used reference materials and daily office supplies within arm's reach of your desk chair. If you have to get up to put something away, chances are you won't.

○ Set up plastic trays or baskets on top of your desk for:
- *Incoming Mail*
- *Outgoing Mail*
- *To Do*
- *To File*

Sort the papers you cleared from your desk into these bins.

○ Go through your To Do pile and let go of "maybe I'll do this someday" projects if you've been holding on to them for a long time.

○ Gather all your sticky notes and form one big To Do list (if you have a Tasks folder on your e-mail, use it). Use only one calendar.

○ Clean out your computer hard drive and delete "cookies" and unwanted files. Defragment your hard drive. (If you do not know how, ask someone to help you.)

○ Toss all those odds and ends in your drawers that are not necessary or useful.

TIPS:

- Keep cords and cables tidy and out of the way by tying garbage bag twists around loose cables behind your computer.

- Empty your Outgoing Mail box each day so you don't forget to mail important documents.

- Don't store mail in your Incoming Mailbox. Open it as soon as possible and sort it into the appropriate bin: To Do, To File, or Trash. Throw the trash away immediately (this includes the envelopes the mail arrived in and any inserts stuffed in with your bills). Put To Do items on your To Do list.

- Take advantage of vertical space to increase your work area. Shelves, cabinets, armoires and plastic paper holders mounted to the wall are all storage solutions.

- If you need more work space for your home office, consider using an extra end table or card table from somewhere in the house.

- If you have papers you need to refer to often, pin them to a bulletin board that is at eye level so they are not messing up your desk.

- Don't waste paper. Buy recycled paper. Whenever possible print on both sides. Keep a basket next to your desk for paper that you are done with. You can use the blank side to jot stuff down or put it in the printer and print on the blank side.

- To save electricity, make sure your computer is set to go into sleep mode whenever you are not using it.

ONCE A MONTH

○ Empty your recycle bin or shred important papers.

○ File the papers in your To File bin.

EVERY 3-6 MONTHS

○ Sort through your To Do pile and get caught up on any projects you've been putting off.

○ Clean out the hard drive on your computer.

ONCE A YEAR

○ Clean out your desk drawers.

○ Go through your files and purge papers you no longer need.

NOTES:

_____

_____

_____

_____

_____

_____

_____

_____

_____

_____

Organize Your Linen Closet

This should be a simple, quick week for you (unless for some reason you have an extra-large linen closet). A linen closet may be used to store bedding, bath and beach towels, tablecloths and extra cleaning supplies. The key to organizing this closet is to arrange all its contents so it can be seen when you open the door. If everything cannot be easily located, chances are you have too much in here and need to start by tossing!

THIS WEEK'S GOALS:

○ Sort through your bath towels, hand towels and washcloths. Toss all that are ripped, ragged or too thin. Fold the remaining towels and place them according to size on a shelf that is accessible to everyone in the house.

○ Sort your sheets, blankets and comforters into three piles: Keep; Donate/Sell and Trash. You only need two sets of sheets for each bed in your house and only one of the sets should be in the linen closet; the other belongs on the bed. (You may have three sets if you like to use flannel sheets in the winter.)

○ Donate or sell sheet sets and blankets that are in good condition but are no longer used. Why let it take up space in your closet when someone else could use it? Trash any that are stained, ripped, worn thin or missing its matching set. Fold and store the remaining sheets in sets on the next highest shelf.

○ Sort all of your remaining items into three categories: Keep, Don't Use, Trash.

○ Toss out the trash and then evaluate your Don't Use pile. It could be full of beauty products you purchased and never used.

○ Unopened items can be donated to a local shelter. Used items are trash, even if you've only used it once. Large items, such as foot baths and hair styling tools, can be sold or donated.

○ Sort your Keep pile into categories, remembering to keep like things together. Designate part or all of a shelf to each category as needed. Put frequently used items on easy-to-reach shelves and surplus items on higher shelves. Possible categories include:
  - *Extra pillows (only a few for guests)*
  - *Beauty supplies*
  - *Extra bathroom supplies (toothpaste, soap—just don't stockpile too much)*
  - *Extra light bulbs*

○ Install hooks on the back of the door to store items such as totes or bathrobes.

NOTES:

_____

_____

_____

_____

_____

_____

_____

_____

_____

_____

_____

TIPS:

- To cut down on laundry and the number of towels your family uses, ask your family members to reuse their bath towels and use only two towels per week. Distinguish between the towels by assigning a different color to each family member so no one complains about using someone else's towel. (This may mean investing in new towels.) Your children may be more excited about this if you let them choose the color of their towels.

- Fold your fitted sheet and flat sheet together and then store them in their matching pillow case. Then you can grab the whole set to be put on the bed with one hand.

- If you will actually use it, keep only one of your "trash" sheets or blankets to use as a picnic blanket.

- You can turn some of your old sheets and towels into cleaning rags by cutting them up. Just be realistic about how many rags you will actually use.

- If you change the décor in a bedroom and buy new linens, decide right away what you will do with the old linens. Donate, sell or trash them. Don't let them become clutter by shoving them in the linen closet.

- Store items that are rarely used, such as comforters, on the top shelf.

- If you have extra space in your bedroom closets, consider storing the bed sheets for that room in there in order to free up space in your linen closet.

- Consider keeping an extra blanket in your vehicle for emergencies.

ONCE A MONTH

Take a few minutes to make sure all of your towels, blankets and linens are nicely folded and stored on the proper shelf. It's easy and tempting to cram items in a closet when you're in a hurry. A few minutes of straightening can save you time in the long run because you'll have an easier time finding things.

EVERY 3-6 MONTHS

Check your surplus bathroom supplies and toss any you haven't gotten around to using in the past few months. Don't replace these items; you don't use them enough to keep extra around. If you buy these items only as needed, you'll save a lot of space in your closet.

ONCE A YEAR

Evaluate the condition of your bath towels, hand towels and washcloths. Toss any that are wearing out. January is a good time to do this to take advantage of the traditional "white" sales in case you need to purchase replacements.

| # Organize Your Basement

How you organize your basement is relative to the type of basement your home has. These days there are a variety of basements in homes—everything from the old dirt-floor basement to full, finished basements that boast playrooms, offices and spare bedrooms. The goal with any basement is to maximize storage space while still protecting your belongings against moisture damage.

My No. 1 rule for keeping a basement organized is to not use this space as a dumping ground for items you can't decide what to do with. If you take the time and energy to store something in your basement, you should be 90 percent sure you are going to use it again.

When you are trying to organize any large storage area, it is helpful to split the area up into zones. A zone is basically a designated section of the space to be a home for "like" things.

THIS WEEK'S GOALS:

○ Sort through all of the items you keep in the basement and make four piles:

    A. Toss (anything broken, moldy or mildewed, and any old trash hidden in the corners)

    B. Sell/Donate (items you never use or no longer want)

    C. Belongs To Someone Else (e.g., grown children)

    D. Keep

○ Discard the Toss pile.

○ Sell or donate the designated items. You could post the item on an Internet auction site or list it in a newspaper.

○ Contact the owner(s) of the Belongs to Someone Else pile and schedule a pickup or delivery date to return the item.

Organize your basement into zones. This will help you keep the room(s) organized and maximize your space. Some ideas for zones may include:

- *Holiday decorations*
- *Play area for the kids*
- *Work area—a tool bench or place to work on home improvements*
- *Storage*
- *Bulky sports equipment*

Do not gather and heap up and store up for yourselves treasures on earth, where moth and rust and worm consume and destroy, and where thieves break through and steal. But gather and heap up and store for yourselves treasures in heaven, where neither moth nor rust nor worm consume and destroy, and where thieves do not break through and steal; For where your treasure is, there will your heart be also.

**—MATTHEW 6:19–21,
AMPLIFIED BIBLE**

Separate the Keep pile into categories. Remember to keep like things together. Possible categories include:

- *Baby items and toys (Keep these only if you plan on having more children.)*
- *Outdoor supplies*
- *Holiday decorations*
- *Clothing*

Evaluate your Keep piles. What are you storing in the basement, and is that really the best place for it? Clothes and toys can mildew (plus it's nearly impossible to remove that dank, musty basement smell). Photos, papers and wood are damaged by the moisture, even if your basement never has standing water. Find a better place to store these items, like a closet or the attic. If the items are worth keeping, they are worth protecting, otherwise they will be ruined and end up in a future toss pile.

○ Evaluate your storage. Do you have enough shelving? Do you have moisture-resistant storage containers? Do you have a storage container for each category? Purchase anything you need.

○ Clearly label the front of each container. Arrange the containers for easy access. Items that are rarely used can go on high shelves or at the bottom of a stack. Frequently used items should be placed in the most convenient area.

TIPS:

- Store items by family member and make each person responsible for his or her own stuff (great for when your grown children move out of your home).

- Only store moisture-resistant items in the basement. Fabrics, papers and even wood can easily be ruined by the high humidity and mildew in basements.

- If you must store fabrics in the basement, store them in vacuum-seal storage bags to reduce the risk of mildew. Make sure the items are freshly washed and toss in a dryer sheet for extra freshness.

- If you use your basement a lot or store a lot of things there, invest in a good dehumidifier.

ONCE A MONTH

○ Check all surfaces for mildew and wipe down the outsides of all storage containers with disinfectant to prevent mildew.

EVERY 3-6 MONTHS

○ Purge holiday decorations and clean out these bins when you decorate for each holiday.

ONCE A YEAR

○ Evaluate what you are storing. Consider tossing, donating or selling anything you haven't used in the past year.

NOTES:

| Organize Your Attic

Attics can be dumping zones for things that a family does not have room for or for things that they don't use but are afraid to part with. Rather than deciding now to part with it, they throw it in the attic so they don't have to look at it. The problem with this way of thinking is that out of sight, out of mind works for only so long. Sooner or later you have to make decisions. And by that time there will be piles and piles of stuff to deal with all at once.

The attic is usually the most difficult room in the house to organize because it entails going upstairs and often requires a pull-down ladder. Before you start, decide on the function of your attic. Is it a place to store unwanted junk or family keepsakes? Many attics are dry, which makes them a more suitable place to store items you want to keep safe for a long time without accessing on a regular basis. While they are dry, attics also are subject to extreme temperatures (very cold in the winter and very hot in the summer), so keep that in mind before you store an item there.

THIS WEEK'S GOALS:

◯ Sort through your items and make four piles:

    A. Toss

    B. Sell/Donate

    C. Belongs To Someone Else

    D. Keep

◯ Discard the Toss pile and move the Sell/Donate and Belongs To Someone Else piles out of the attic.

◯ Separate the Keep pile into categories. Possibilities include:

- *Toys/baby items*
- *Clothing*
- *Holiday decorations*
- *Heirlooms/memorabilia*

> *But godliness with content-ment is great gain. For we brought nothing into the world, and we can take nothing out of it.*
>
> **—I TIMOTHY 6:6-7, NEW INTERNATIONAL VERSION**

Be honest about what you need to keep. If it's not a seasonal item and it's in the attic, you're not using it, so do you really need it? If you can use it now, move it out of the attic and put it to use. Is there someone else in your family who would cherish or use the heirlooms and memorabilia you're storing in your attic? Consider giving these items away.

○ When appropriate, break the Keep categories down further by holiday, season or family member (especially for decorations and clothing). This makes it easier to find what you are looking for when you need it.

○ Remove any items that can be damaged by the extreme heat.

○ Place each category in its own plastic bin or bins and label the side of each container. Store photographs and important documents in fireproof containers.

○ Arrange the bins by category, keeping frequently used items in the easiest-to-reach places. Stack bins to make the most of your space. If you have so many bins that you can't easily move through the attic, then you need to toss more!

○ Make arrangements to sell or donate the appropriate items.

○ Contact the owner(s) of the Belongs To Someone Else pile and schedule a pickup date. This may be a grown child who no longer lives with you.

TIPS:

- In the future, ask yourself these questions before you shove something in the attic:

  What is the real reason I am keeping this?

  Will it remain in the same condition in the attic?

  If I can't see it, how will I remember I have it?

  Honestly, will I ever go up to the attic to get this item again?

  Do I love this?

- Organize your attic into zones. This will help you keep the area organized and maximize your space. Ideas for zones may include:

  Memorabilia

  Holiday decorations

  Out-of-season clothing

  Outgrown kids' items

- Store items by family member and make each person responsible for his or her own things (this is great for when grown children move out of your home).

- Lay down plywood or sheets if the floor is not in good condition.

- Loose items waste space and are hard to safeguard. Use clear containers for storage so that items can be easily located.

- Containers and boxes are easier to get to if they are on shelves.

- Take advantage of the roof slope by mounting a pole between roof rafters for out-of-season clothing. Store clothing in zippered garment bags.

ONCE A MONTH

◯ Peek in the attic to make sure nothing is being ruined by heat or animals. And while you are up there, grab two things you could toss!

EVERY 3–6 MONTHS

◯ Anytime you use your holiday decorations, get rid of items you don't use that year. If you don't use it, don't keep it.

◯ If you have attic windows open them on a nice day to air out this space.

ONCE A YEAR

◯ Tighten the hardware on your pull-down attic stairway if you have one.

◯ Donate or sell any clothing that hasn't left the attic in the past year. If you didn't wear it this year, you won't wear it next year.

NOTES:

_____

_____

_____

_____

_____

_____

_____

Organize Your Garage

Oh, the garage! I let my husband handle this area of our house. It is the one room he actually loves to organize! Is it a dream of yours to pull your car into a clean, organized garage at the end of a long day? You can make that dream a reality with a little organizing and maybe a lot of tossing. If you currently cannot fit your vehicle in the garage, you probably have too much stuff. Consider tossing, selling or storing extras you must keep in a separate storage shed.

The obvious functions of your garage are parking and storage for garden supplies, outdoor toys, sports equipment and pet accessories. But if your garage is organized and open, you'll also have a covered area for outdoor parties at your home, a place to work on your vehicle and a play area for your children during bad weather.

THIS WEEK'S GOALS:

○ Empty your garage of all its contents. You may want to get a few storage containers to house items outside when you empty your garage. As you remove items, sort them into these general piles:

- *Trash (broken items, rusty objects, etc.)*
- *Belongs In The Garage*
- *Doesn't Belong In The Garage*
- *Sell/Donate*
- *Borrowed From Someone Else, and needs to be returned*

○ Place all of the trash in waste containers. Move the Borrowed and Doesn't Belong categories to a holding area outside of the garage. You'll deal with them later; don't get sidetracked.

○ Once the garage is empty, pull your car(s) in and park there. This lets you see just how much storage room you have in the garage. Put tape around the car's perimeter to mark where it will sit, then remove the car so it won't be in your way as you return items to the garage.

○ Sort the Belongs In Garage items by category: power tools, lawn equipment, lawn furniture, toys, sports equipment and seasonal storage. Will everything fit in the garage with the car parked there? If not, you may need to purge more.

○ Designate areas for each category, and label the areas as such. Use your wall space as much as possible. Think height to hang up tools, rakes, bikes, fishing poles, snow shovels. You may need to buy and install hooks and brackets. Also use shelves for vertical storage. Store loose, small tools in a toolbox.

○ If everything fits, congratulations! If not, you'll need to get creative. Is there anything else you can donate or sell? Is there a category that could be stored somewhere else, such as the basement or attic? Make sure you have room in the new storage area before you place a category there. You should know exactly where it will fit before you move it, otherwise you've simply dumped the clutter somewhere else instead of removing it.

○ Now it's time to deal with the Doesn't Belong In The Garage pile. Be honest, do you really use this stuff? If so, why is it in the garage and not where it belongs? Sort everything into three basic categories: Keep, Donate, Sell. If you don't use it, get rid of it.

○ Now go through your Keep pile and decide the best home for each item. Don't just name a room; try to find a specific place within the room so it has a real home. Then distribute the items to their new homes.

○ Contact the owners of any items you borrowed and arrange a time to return the items.

○ Make arrangements to get your donated items to the proper charity. You also can sit large, weather-resistant items out in your yard with a "free" sign and see if anyone picks them up. If it's not gone within a week, make other arrangements.

○ Start selling items (see pages 20-21 for suggestions). If you are having a yard sale, it's okay to store the sale items until you've reached all your organizing goals and are ready for the sale.

TIPS:

- Use open shelves to store everyday items and cabinets to keep less attractive items out of sight.

- Every garage needs some sort of workbench so you have an area to work on home improvements and basic fix-its. If your garage is small, consider a drop-down or fold-down bench.

- Store flammable liquids such as gasoline, paint thinner, turpentine and cleaning supplies in metal containers with tight caps.

- Place all chemicals and dangerous items on high shelves so that children and pets cannot get to them.

- Store children's toys close to the ground so they can reach them on their own. Consider giving your kids their own area in the garage to store their items so they know where to find their toys and sports equipment and where to return them when they are done.

- Label all containers, especially if they are not clear containers, so you know the contents at a glance. Color code when necessary based on category or family member.

- To increase the lighting in your garage, paint the ceiling with light-colored, high gloss paint.

- Hang tools on a Peg-Board in the garage. Use a marker to trace the outline of the tool on the board so everyone knows where each tool belongs.

STAY ORGANIZED!

ONCE A MONTH

○ Sweep out the garage. Clean up any oil spots.

EVERY 3–6 MONTHS

○ Check your lawn equipment, lawn furniture, toys and other garage items each season. Toss damaged or worn items and donate or sell things that you've stopped using.

ONCE A YEAR

○ Check the screws and nuts on the overhead garage door and the auto reverse functions.

○ Thoroughly clean the entire garage.

Organize Your Yard & Garden

Your yard creates a visitor's first impression of your home. It is also the one part of your personal space that can be seen by anyone who drives or walks by—even those not invited. My family takes their yards and gardens very seriously. It seems I have been surrounded by green thumbs my entire life. So, when my husband and I purchased our first home, I also took our new yard very seriously. After pouring lots of money and plants into the landscaping, I learned many things: Don't plant anything you don't have time to care for; perennials are my friend; and it is a lot harder to dig in the North Carolina clay than it is in upstate New York dirt! My best advice for organizing your yard and garden is to keep in mind how much time you'll have to spend in this area in the future. Don't plant more than you can maintain.

THIS WEEK'S GOALS:

○ Survey your yard and garden. Gather up all the trash. Toss:
- *Rusty, old tools*
- *Hammocks with holes*
- *Broken fencing*
- *Brush piles and dead plants*
- *Pieces of broken swing sets*
- *Leftover piles of rocks, sand, or wood*
- *Broken or badly weathered decorations*

○ Hose down all of your window screens and wash the windows.

○ Clean out the gutters and downspouts.

○ Pull weeds and then weed-and-feed your garden.

○ Rake the leaves and trim any unruly bushes.

○ Till your garden.

○ Put out a new welcome mat.

○ Sweep porches and decks.
Toss:
  - *Leftover items under the porch or deck*
  - *Molding flower pots*
  - *Broken lawn furniture*

○ If you have a pool, check the chemical balance and make sure you are properly caring for it. Create a regular schedule for maintenance by designating one hour a week to pool care.

○ Schedule time for any large exterior projects you may have (planting a new flower bed, repairing the deck, planting a tree). Write these work dates in your day planner and on the family calendar. If you don't plan it, it won't happen!

A garden is a lot like life. Neglect the little things and it will deteriorate into chaos. Tend to the little things and it will become a thing of beauty.

**—MARIA GRACIA,
FINALLY ORGANIZED,
FINALLY FREE**

TIPS:

- Before you plant your garden and flower beds, make a colored sketch to check the layout and design. This can help you select the most attractive flowers for your yard.

- Water in the late evening or very early morning so the sun doesn't evaporate the moisture before it soaks through the soil.

- Schedule a yard-work day at the end of each season to take care of all your seasonal responsibilities (till the garden, put lawn/patio furniture in storage, install storm windows) at one time.

- Instead of raking up leaves in autumn, mow over them with a bagging mower. All of the leaves will be removed from the yard and the clippings make great compost for your garden.

- Pegged coat racks are great to hang in a shed for tools and supplies that have looped strings or cords. These pegged racks are also great by a pool to dry wet towels.

- Shop Thursdays and Fridays for your plants and gardening supplies to get the best selection.

- If you have no space or time for a separate vegetable garden, sprinkle a few veggie plants in your flower beds.

STAY ORGANIZED!

ONCE A MONTH

◯ Weed and fertilize your garden and flower beds.

EVERY 3–6 MONTHS

◯ Prepare your yard and home exterior for the upcoming season.

◯ Tidy up the edges of your flower beds.

◯ Fertilize your yard.

ONCE A YEAR

◯ Clean your gutters and downspouts.

◯ Spread new mulch as needed.

◯ Stain your fence and deck.

◯ Sharpen your mower blade.

Organize Your Special Events

Organize Your Holiday

Holidays are meant to be a time of celebration, not a time to run around tired, stressed out and moody! We've all had our moments—those times when you feel you will never be able to accomplish everything that needs to be done. My suggestion is to imagine how you would ideally like to spend the holidays and then make it happen. Do not be pressured to spend it the way society and family expect you to. For ideas on how to do this listen to "No More Christmas Clutter" on my website.

THIS WEEK'S GOALS:

○ Decide what holidays and events are important for you to celebrate. Mark them on your calendar. If you decorate for the holidays, decide when you want to start decorating and when you want to take down the decorations. Mark these dates on your calendar as well.

○ Gather all your interior decorations for all holidays and put them in one place. Sort through them and organize by holiday. Each holiday should have its own separate storage container (or containers) that is clearly labeled. If space is an issue, place decorations in labeled shoeboxes and place those boxes in a larger storage container. This lets you fit more than one holiday in the large container and still keep the items separate and easy to access. As you sort, toss anything that is broken. Keep only the decorations you use and love.

○ Find the best place to store all of your interior decorations. This may mean cleaning out a closet or clearing space in the attic.

○ Repeat Goals 2 and 3 with your exterior decorations.

There is a time for every-
thing, and a season for ev-
ery activity under heaven.

—ECCLESIASTES 3:1
NEW INTERNATIONAL VERSION

○ Prioritize and plan your gift- and card-giving. Decide the date you want to have your shopping finished and the date you want to have your cards sent out. Mark these goals on your calendar.

○ Gather all of your wrapping paper (holiday, birthday, any occasion) and gift bags. Store them in an accessible drawer or bin.

○ Keep track of everyone's birthday or anniversary by:
  - writing it on your planner in January
  - adding it to your phone calendar and setting an alert
  - signing up for a free online reminder service like www.birthdayalarm.com

○ Send gift certificates for presents. It really simplifies things—no shopping, wrapping, or exchanges.

○ Shop for gifts all year round at sales. Only do this if you have the room to store the gifts. Don't hide gifts all over the house; you'll forget where they are. Have one location for them all. Keep a list of what you buy so you don't forget and don't over shop.

○ Organize greeting cards in an accordian file based on occasion.

TIPS:

- Keep it simple. Don't let minor details cause you to forget to celebrate the real meaning of the holiday. You don't need perfection.

- Take time on each holiday to live in the moment and be grateful.

- We all need the reassurance and comforts of family traditions. Give yourself time to enjoy them.

- When possible, involve your children and your spouse in your holiday planning.

- Always test your holiday lights before you string them up.

- Keep an updated mailing list on your computer so that you can print address labels when mailing greeting cards.

- When you decorate for a holiday, immediately purge all decorations you do not use. If you are not using it, there must be a reason—most likely you don't like it!

Reuse gift bags!

Reduce the amount of merchandise coming into your home during the holidays by requesting that family and friends give giftcards or money, or make a donation to your favorite charity instead of purchasing a gift item for you.

Ask family and friends to give you or your children experiences instead of things at the holidays. Trips, tickets and lessons are all great ideas and don't add clutter to your home.

Let your creativity make up for where money lacks. Remember, the point of a holiday is to let others know how much they are loved and appreciated—not to impress them. A homemade gift can mean more than an expensive one.

ONCE A MONTH

◯ On the first of the month, make note of any birthdays or holidays that will be celebrated that month. Set deadlines for buying any necessary presents, planning parties, mailing cards and setting up/taking down decorations.

EVERY 3–6 MONTHS

◯ Purge your unused holiday decorations as soon as you are finished decorating for that holiday.

$ Stock up on holiday wrapping paper during sales. Purchase Christmas paper at the end-of-the-season sales for the following year so you can start wrapping early.

ONCE A YEAR

◯ Record all your important holiday dates in your yearly planner.

NOTES:

_____

_____

_____

_____

_____

_____

_____

_____

_____

_____

Organize Your Party

A party is a time for celebration! It's usually a time to spend with family and friends. Unfortunately, many of us put so much emphasis on planning the "perfect" party and worrying about what our guests will think, we end up stressed out and lose focus on what is most important—having fun and making memories. The most important thing to remember when planning a party—whether it's a bridal shower or a birthday—is don't procrastinate. Anything you can get done before the actual day of the party will make your life much easier and your party much more enjoyable. Once the guests arrive, take a deep breath and have fun! You probably won't need to put these goals into practice until you have a party to plan. Let these goals be a reference anytime you need to prepare for a special event.

THIS WEEK'S GOALS:

◯ Pick a date.

◯ Decide on your guest list.

◯ If the party will not be held at your house, schedule time to call and visit possible venues.

◯ Plan your menu. Get out any recipes you plan to serve and make a complete grocery list. Break the list down into two categories—nonperishable and perishable. You can buy all of the nonperishable items well in advance and pick up the perishable food a day or two before the party so it's fresh.

◯ Write invitations and mail them. Or save yourself time and money by sending virtual invitations at websites such as www.punchbowl.com or www.evite.com. These sites will keep track of RSVPs for you! Make sure invites are sent two to six weeks before the event, depending on the type of party.

○ Choose the theme and decorations. Remember, it's your party, so select a theme that fits your personality and makes all of your effort fun!

○ Decide if you will give your guests favors. If yes, decide what kind and schedule time in your planner to pick them up. If you will make the favors yourself, schedule time to work on them.

○ Decide what activities or games you want to include, if any.

○ Give your house a good cleaning the day before if the party is being held at your home.

○ Decorate and prepare as much food as possible the day before the party.

NOTES:

_____
_____
_____
_____
_____
_____
_____
_____
_____
_____
_____

TIPS:

- When you receive an invitation to a party, write down the time, address and phone number in your planner immediately. If you have never been there before, include directions. Remember to RSVP!! Don't be a procrastinator.

- Premade party trays from the grocery, deli, or bakery save tons of food prep time.

- Dress early for your party to make sure you are calm and looking good before the first guest arrives.

- Greet each one of your guests in person.

- Always request RSVPs from guests for any party you host. You'll know exactly how much food to buy, and you'll be able to arrange adequate seating for your guests.

- Plan your menu before you send out invitations. Then, if any of your guests offer to bring a dish, you can tell them what to bring.

NOTES:

_____

_____

_____

_____

_____

_____

_____

_____

_____

_____

PARTY CHECKLIST

○ Set Up

  __ Tablecloths

  __ Plates: large, small

  __ Bowls

  __ Cups: pop, coffee, wine

  __ Napkins/paper towels

  __ Plastic utensils

  __ Garbage bags

  __ Tape

  __ Scissors

  __ Coolers

  __ Can opener

  __ Extension cords

  __ Pot holders

  __ Washcloths/dish towels

  __ Coffeemaker

  __ Bug spray/sunscreen (if the event is outside)

  __ Knives to cut rolls

  __ Plastic containers

○ Food

  __ Main dish

  __ Rolls

  __ Salads

  __ Sides

  __ Dessert

  __ Beverages

  __ Ice

  __ Condiments/dressings

  __ Salt and pepper

Organize Your Trip

The purpose of taking a vacation is to have fun, relax, and refresh. Trying to do too much when you return can undermine what you've gained by getting away. Take time to plan before you leave, and slow down when you return. You will make the transition from vacation to "regular life" a lot easier, and the benefits of your vacation will last much longer.

THIS WEEK'S GOALS:

○ Decide on your form of transportation. If you plan to fly, the best travel days are Tuesday, Wednesday and Saturday. Try to book flights twenty-one days in advance. Avoid booking the last flight of the day, so that if it gets cancelled you won't be stranded.

○ If necessary, apply for a passport and schedule immunizations several months in advance of your trip. On average, it takes ten to twelve weeks for the government to process your passport request. Some vaccines are administered in stages that are weeks apart, so be sure you have enough time to complete all of the stages before you leave for your trip.

○ Write your address on the inside and the outside of your luggage. Attach something personal (such as a distinctive ribbon or sticker) to each piece of your luggage to make it recognizable on a luggage carousel. This will also cut down on the chance of someone else mistaking it for his.

○ Pack a fabric laundry bag. Keep your dirty laundry in it while you are on your trip, and when the trip is over, pack it in

When preparing to travel,
lay out all your clothes and
all your money. Then take
half the clothes and twice
the money.

—SUSAN HELLER

○ your suitcase to keep dirty clothes separate.

○ When you schedule vacation time from work, be sure to save one vacation day to recover at home.

○ Plan out your stay before you pack. For lighter packing, stick to three or four colors of clothing. This is the simplest way to maximize the clothing that you take. Make sure that many of the articles can be worn with each other. Only pack 50 percent of what you want to take. If there are a few "just in case" items you are not sure about, consider purchasing them where you are going if you happen to need them.

○ Purchase and pack travel-size toiletries. Transfer items such as your facial cleanser into small plastic bottles. Any liquids you must take should be in tightly sealed plastic containers, filled only three-fourths of the way, and put in secured plastic bags. Squeeze excess air from bottles and tubes so that they'll be less likely to leak.

○ Clean your house before you leave so you can come back to a welcoming, clutter-free home. You'll feel more relaxed when you return from your trip.

○ In case of emergency, email a copy of your itinerary to a friend or family member who is not traveling with you.

○ Use a lightweight bag to carry items that you will need to access while traveling to your destination—such as tickets, money, driver's license, passport (for foreign trips), medicines, camera, eyeglasses, cell phone, reading material and important papers.

○ Leave a key to your home with a family member or friend. Set up responsibility for your pets and plants.

○ Confirm flight information and departure time if you are flying. If you are driving, make sure you have a good app on your phone that will help with directions and road conditions. I personally love the apps: Flightstats for flying and Waze for driving.

○ The night before your trip, place suitcases, tickets, purse or wallet, and photo ID near the door. If you're traveling by car, load as much as you can the night before.

○ Remove perishables from the refrigerator, empty all of your wastebaskets and take out the garbage.

○ Lock all windows and doors and activate the alarm system.

TIPS:

- Download all photos from your phone to your computer to save space and in case you were to loose your phone.

- Pack socks, underwear and belts in your shoes to save space.

- If you are traveling with children, pack toys and games to keep them occupied.

- Bring an extra suitcase if you plan on doing a lot of shopping.

- When purchasing luggage be sure to choose the one best for the type of travel you do most often. Also, look for luggage made of lightweight material and 360 wheels.

- As you pack your suitcase, pack last what you'll need first so it will be easy to access when you arrive.

- If you are traveling by plane, don't pack your valuables in your suitcase. Always keep them in your carry-on.

- Make a list of everything you pack and take the list with you on your trip. Use it when repacking for the return trip home so you don't leave anything behind.

- The week before you leave, cook a healthy meal, such as chili or soup, and double the ingredients. Eat half and freeze the rest so you'll have an easy meal to heat up when you return.

- When you return, make the most of your vacation day at home. Let your voicemail answer the phone. Turn the ringer off, if it's too tempting! Fully unpack, do the laundry and process the mail. Check voicemail and e-mail only after you get your home back in order or you'll get distracted and frustrated. Rest. Return to your exercise routine, take a walk, or work in the garden. Sleep late, take a nap, or finish the book you started on vacation.

- 💲 Unplug small appliances and electronics before you leave. They continue to draw electricity even if they are turned off.

- If you need to enter through US customs in your travels the Mobile Passport app is a huge time saver!

- Write down all your credit card numbers along with the phone number to call in case they are stolen while you are on your trip and you need to cancel them as quickly as possible.

PACKING LIST FOR ADULTS

___ Photo ID

___ Clothes

___ Undergarments, sleepwear

___ Belts

___ Socks and shoes

___ Ties

___ Jackets, hats, gloves, umbrella

___ Toothpaste, toothbrushes

___ Makeup, cotton balls/cotton swabs

___ Perfume, lotion, deodorant

___ Razor, tweezers

___ Bathing suit

___ Beach towels

___ Sunscreen

___ Hair dryer/curling iron/clips

___ Camera, batteries

___ Video camera

___ Money/credit and debit cards

___ Invitation/directions

___ Address book

___ Mobile phone, phone charger

___ Presents/cards to give

___ Borrowed items to give back

___ Book/magazine

___ Corkscrew

___ Gum

___ Electrical converter (if necessary)

___ Fabric bag for dirty laundry

PACKING LIST FOR KIDS

___ Outfits
___ Pajamas
___ Socks
___ Shoes
___ Jacket
___ Hats
___ Bathing suit
___ Swimming gear
___ Sunscreen
___ Medicines
___ Diapers, diaper ointment
___ Wipes
___ Baby food
___ Formula
___ Bottles
___ Spoons
___ Bibs
___ Favorite toys
___ Books
___ Videos
___ Stroller

Organize Your Move

Whether you are moving down the street or across the country, moving is a time-consuming and monumental event. The tips and checklist below are designed to keep you organized, on task and stress-free before, during and after your move.

THIS WEEK'S GOALS:

○ As soon as you decide to move, start sorting through all your belongings and donate or trash items you don't want to take with you. This will save you time and space when packing and will give you a fresh, clutter-free start in your new home. Don't move and then sort. You may want to approach this job room by room, tackling one area each day or week, depending on how much time you have. Start sooner rather than later.

○ Take pictures of your current home before you pack so you will remember what you have.

○ Pack by room, filling each box with items from only one room. Label the box with the appropriate room, then number each box you pack with a permanent marker. List the numbers of each box in a notebook. Write the contents of each box next to the appropriate number.

○ Pack all decorations and non-necessity items (anything you can live without until you move) first. If you are selling your home, remove as many personal items as possible for showings. Homebuyers want to picture their own belongings in the space.

○ Pack heavy items in small boxes that are not overfilled so they are easier to lift. Pack light things in larger boxes.

It pays to plan ahead.
It wasn't raining when Noah
built the ark.

—ANONYMOUS

○ Pack your clothes in large wardrobe boxes or hang them from a temporary rod in the back of your vehicle, and save yourself tons of time by not having to re-hang, wash, iron, etc.

○ Pack your books in the order they appear on the current shelves.

○ When moving into your new home, place all boxes in a spare room in piles according the category: kitchen, bath, etc. Then pull one box at a time to unpack. This will make unpacking a lot less overwhelming, and you will be able to move around your new place easier.

❧ Don't just throw away all those boxes after you moved. Recycle by giving them to a friend who will be moving or giving them to a local moving company.

💲 Move less stuff to save more money on movers and gas and to save more time on unloading and unpacking.

NOTES:

_____

_____

_____

_____

_____

_____

◯   6-12 Weeks Prior:

___ Start a box of items that can be donated or go into a yard sale. Search room by room for items you don't use or don't want to take with you.

___ If necessary, set a date for a yard sale or auction.

___ Start collecting boxes and asking family, friends and acquaintances to save their boxes for you.

___ Save all plastic bags you get while shopping. These are great for packing!

___ Start making a list of all the places that should be notified of your address change (watch your mail).

___ Call and get quotes from moving companies and truck rental places.

___ Order new address labels and checks.

___ Contact your insurance company to make changes.

___ If your children will be changing schools, contact both their new school about enrollment and their old school about transferring records.

___ Get doctor and vet records.

___ Order an ID tag for your pet with your new address on it.

___ Make sure your address book is updated with information for everyone you are leaving behind.

MOVING CHECKLIST

○ 2-5 Weeks Prior:

__ Start packing everything you will not need in the next five weeks. Do not pack anything that you have not used in the last year! (Donate, sell, or trash these items.)

__ Number each box and label the room it belongs in. Then keep a log of exactly what is in each box. This will save you time hunting for items later on.

__ Begin using up food and supplies.

__ Arrange to have the utilities turned on at your new residence.

__ Cancel your paper delivery.

○ 1 Week Prior:

__ Send out change of address cards.

__ Visit the post office or www.usps.com to complete a change of address form.

__ Wash and pack curtains.

__ Call for a phone book to be delivered to your new home.

__ Pick up dry cleaning.

__ Defrost freezer.

○ Organize After You Are Moved In:

__ Change your address on your driver's license.

__ Enroll children in school.

__ Make a list of new emergency numbers.

__ Check with the post office to see if any mail is being held for you.

__ Register your vehicles.

Organize Back-To-School Time

If you are organized at back-to-school time, your next nine months will run much smoother. When the new school year dawns, it is just as important for parents to organize their responsibilities as it is for them to get their children organized and prepared.

THIS WEEK'S GOALS:

○ Schedule any doctor appointments your child needs.

○ At least four weeks before school starts, organize your child's closet and bedroom. Take inventory of what clothes still fit and what replacements are needed. Shop for back-to-school clothes.

○ Determine any before or after school care you may need and make the proper arrangements.

○ Designate a "school information zone" in your house where you can post school announcements, trip slips, etc. This is also a great place to post a family calendar so all family members know what to expect in the upcoming days. Transfer all relevant information from your child's school calendar onto the family calendar so everything is in one place; you'll avoid double-booked appointments and activities.

○ Designate a location where your children can do their homework without being easily distracted. Sort and organize the child's homework station. Clear out old paperwork from the previous school year and make room for this year's papers.

○ Designate a Launch Pad where each family member can store all the things needed on a daily basis for school or work, such

*Don't limit a child to your
own learning, for he was
born in another time.*

—RABBINICAL SAYING

as backpacks, coats, lunch boxes, laptops, and shoes (see Week 53). Use hooks, cubbies, a closet, or a chest of drawers to store and organize items in this zone. Whether this area is near the doorway or in a mudroom, it will prevent family members from throwing everything in a pile when they walk in the door.

○ Hold a family meeting to discuss all upcoming aspects of the new school year. Be sure to discuss:
- *Morning/nighttime routines*
- *Changes in the family's weekly schedule*
- *Expectations*
- *Responsibilities: chores, changes in responsibilities*
- *Implement or refresh safety rules for the bus stop or walking to school (e.g., Stranger Danger)*
- *Concerns such as your child going to school for the first time, or starting a new school or getting a new teacher. (Ask him if he has any questions or concerns and address them now.)*

○ Help your children's bodies adjust to the new school year schedule by setting and following the school-night bedtime and school-day wake-up time two or three weeks before school begins. This way your children can be properly rested from the very beginning of the school year.

○ Practice the morning school routine with younger children before the first day of school. Have a set schedule and consequences for being late.

○ Fill out and hand in any paperwork necessary for after-school activities such as sports, music lessons, dance, or scouts.

○ Set up a binder for important school papers you may need to refer to later. Add papers as you receive them. Use colored dividers for each child. Empty this at the end of the school year.

○ Purchase back-to-school supplies and pick up extras for later in the year. Include supplies needed for extracurricular activities.

○ The night before the first day of school, make sure your camera and video recorders have fresh, fully charged batteries so you can easily record the memories.

○ Create a homework chart and display it in your school zone. This chart may be a dry erase board or a simple calendar. Each day when your child gets home, mark on the homework chart what needs to be done before the next day of school.

TIPS:

- If you don't have space in your mudroom to create a family Launch Pad, consider revamping a hall closet. Install hooks your children can easily reach.

- Before you start shopping for back-to-school clothes, go through the hand-me-down garments you've been saving to see if any will fit your child this year.

- Put your TV and video games on an automatic timer. The kind used for Christmas lights works for this, or you can purchase a more advanced model that allows you to program time allowances based on the day of the week. Use a parental control app for other electronic devices.

- Save time in the morning by laying out your child's clothes the night before. If your child is old enough to dress himself, have him lay out his own clothes. You can even use a shallow storage container under the bed and divide it by each day of the week.

- Create a visual chart of what your child needs to do in the morning for school (for example: a picture of brushing teeth, getting dressed or brushing hair). Draw the pictures, clip them from magazines or take a picture of your child completing the task. Post the chart behind the bathroom door or in her bedroom so she can be self-sufficient.

- Play music in the house while everyone is getting ready to make the mood light and happy. Leave the TV off to avoid distractions.

BACK-TO-SCHOOL CHECKLIST

___ Book bag

___ Pencils/pens

___ Scissors

___ Lunch box

___ Folders

___ School paperwork

___ Notebook paper

___ Clothes

___ Shoes

___ Jackets

___ Umbrella

___ Sports equipment

___ Accessories and equipment for extracurricular activities

Organize Your Pregnancy

You're pregnant—congratulations and welcome to parenthood, an emotional, exciting, difficult, rewarding ride!

I truly believe what Vicki Iovine writes in her book The Girlfriends' Guide to Pregnancy: "The world loves a pregnant woman, because we all want to protect her and encourage her, and other women who had babies are ecstatic to have a new member joining her ranks."

In my own experience both as a mother and in operating two businesses that cater to moms, I have come to one conclusion: Deep down, all moms are essentially the same. We love our children; we want what is best for our children...and we are constantly cleaning up after our children! You should already be preparing for the cleaning-up part when your nesting instincts start kicking in. Take advantage of this extra motivation and energy because this is a great time to get caught up before baby arrives. The more you can accomplish now, the more time you will have to spend with your baby once he or she arrives.

THIS WEEK'S GOALS:

○ Register for baby items. Don't forget to include toiletries, diapers and medicines. When registering for the first time, try to choose products that will endure at least two children, if not more. (You may not get a baby shower next time!) It is better to go with neutral colors for items such as cribs, strollers and car seats.

○ Get your To Do lists out of the way now. Include major projects you will not have time for once the baby arrives. Do not procrastinate on thank-you cards from baby showers. If you

*A new baby is like the
beginning of all things—
wonder, hope, a dream of
possibilities.*

—EDNA J. LE SHAN

send these out immediately, you don't have to think about it again.

○ Review your health insurance plan so you know what you are getting for your money.

○ If you have to return to work after your baby is born, use this time to interview child-care providers so that you don't waste too much time doing this once the baby is here. If you are using a daycare, call to get your name on the list at least six months before your baby is due.

○ Start stocking up on diapers!

○ Have a plan to organize the memories and keepsakes you collect during this special time:
  - *Use a cute, keepsake box to organize all cards and notes you receive.*
  - *Place all your pregnancy and baby shower pictures in one photo album.*
  - *See Week 32 for more ideas.*

○ Research birthing classes and register for them at least a month before your due date.

○ As you get closer to your due date, start cooking meals and freezing them so you don't have to worry about cooking once the baby arrives.

○ Start baby-proofing the house.
  - *Make sure window blind cords are out of reach from the crib and changing table. Consider installing cordless blinds and curtains.*

> - *Place bumper pads on sharp corners of furniture.*
> - *Secure all bookshelves to walls so little ones cannot pull them over.*
> - *Try crib sheets on to make sure they fit securely.*
>
> ○ Discuss with your partner who you want at the hospital or in the delivery room. Then make your wishes clear to your family. Stick with your decision no matter who tries to persuade you differently.

TIPS:

- Schedule time for visitors: This gives loved ones more one-on-one time with the baby, and you won't feel so overwhelmed. Make sure you have enough time alone with the baby, too!

- Take lots of pictures!

- After the baby is born, avoid drop-in visitors when you are sleeping by putting a friendly note on the door. Also, let relatives and friends know the baby's schedule so they don't interrupt naps or feeding times.

- Don't save maternity clothes for more than three years. They do go out of style.

REGISTRY CHECKLIST

(The items on this list are only recommendations.)

___ Crib

___ Mattress

___ Bassinet

___ Portable crib

___ Sheets

___ Dresser

___ Rocking chair or glider

___ Changing table

___ Changing pad

___ Changing pad cover

___ High chair

___ Stationary play circle

___ Walker

___ Diaper bag

___ Car seat (infant and booster)

___ Stroller

___ Onesies

___ Wipe warmer

___ Bottles

___ Towels/washcloths

___ Blankets

___ Bedding

___ Monitor

___ Mobile

___ Sound machine

___ Diaper bin

___ Bathtub

___ Ointment

___ Thermometer

___ Breast pump

___ Bouncy seat

___ Bumbo seat

___ Swing

___ Bibs

___ Car seat cover

NOTES:

_____

_____

_____

_____

_____

_____

_____

| Organize Your Nursery

Before you plan and organize your nursery, decide what tasks you will be doing there. Will you use this area to change diapers, feed, dress, rock, snuggle and read to the baby? Will baby take naps in the nursery? Designate areas of the room where each activity will be performed. You can read, snuggle and rock at the same time, so place a bookshelf or a basket of books near a glider. Changing and dressing occur simultaneously, so store diapers, lotion and ointment near the clothing.

THIS WEEK'S GOALS:

○ Decide on the décor and furniture for the nursery. Purchase furniture with suitable storage that can be used for dual purposes. You can place a changing pad atop a dresser and eliminate your need for a changing table. Consider purchasing a crib that converts to a toddler bed. In the long run this will save you money (you'll get more use out of the bed, thus getting more for your money), time (you won't waste time shopping for and assembling another bed) and space (you won't have to store a crib).

○ Set dates to paint the room, assemble furniture and install a smoke detector in or near the room. Make sure your nursery is set up no less than a month before the baby is due. You want to be prepared in case the baby arrives early!

○ Place a low-wattage lamp or dimmer switch in the nursery for those nights when you want just enough light to change and feed the baby without causing a lot of distraction.

○ Use shelves to display books, toys, photographs and other keepsakes.

○ Whether you use a glider or the recliner in the family room, make sure you have a comfortable and convenient place to feed your baby.

○ Evaluate your nursery closet. Buy any organizing system necessary to maximize your space. (See Week 34 for more ideas.)

○ Pack the diaper bag before you go into labor.

NOTES:

_____

_____

_____

_____

_____

_____

_____

_____

_____

_____

_____

_____

_____

_____

_____

_____

_____

TIPS:

- Purchase furniture that is baby-safe—made with nontoxic paint or stain, with smooth and rounded knobs and corners.

- Crib slats should be no more than $2^3/_8$ inches (6cm) apart.

- Hang an over-the-door shoe organizer with multiple pockets on the back of the closet door to keep all the small items organized. This gives you quick access to the items and makes it easy to put them away.

- Keep a plastic bin on the floor of the closet. When your baby outgrows something, you can toss it in there until it is time to donate or sell. Try hanging a second rod in the closet for extra space.

- After you choose a nursery theme, give yourself a few weeks, or better, a couple of months, to let it really sink in before you rush out and buy every piece of the matching nursery set or every theme-related item you can get your hands on. If after this time period you still love the theme, go for it. • Aft

- Shop your local kids consignment sales before you pay full price.

NOTES:

_____
_____
_____
_____
_____
_____
_____

DIAPER BAG CHECKLIST

These items are handy to carry at all times:

Changing:

__ Diapers

__ Wipes in travel
    container

__ Plastic grocery
    bag

__ Diaper-rash
    ointment

__ Plastic changing
    mat

__ Lotion

Dressing:

__ Two outfits

__ Onesies

__ Socks

__ Two bibs

__ Blanket

__ Burping cloth

__ Hat

__ Sunglasses

__ Mittens, jacket

Feeding:

__ Baby food

__ Formula

__ Snacks

__ Bottled water

Extras:

__ Two pacifiers

__ Toys

__ Teething rings

__ Sunscreen

__ Medicines

__ Gas drops

__ Snack for Mom

__Hand sanitizer

Organize Your Family's Safety Plan

Your family's safety should be your top priority. Make time in your hectic life to complete each goal listed this week. We can't plan for emergencies, but we can prepare for and possibly prevent them. This may seem like a simple week, but please don't put off these tasks—you could end up being a day late.

THIS WEEK'S GOALS:

○ Check your smoke alarm batteries and check all fire extinguishers to make sure they are not expired.

○ Formulate a fire safety plan with your family. Each member should have two exit routes for his or her bedroom. Create a central meeting place, such as a tree in the front yard or backyard, in case of a fire.

○ Create a home inventory list of the valuables in your home. You can also video each room of your house and take pictures for your records in case of theft or fire.

○ Check your water heater and make sure it is not set higher than 120°F (49°C).

○ Check all lamps and lighting fixtures and make sure the bulbs in them are the correct wattage.

○ Write down emergency phone numbers and place them near your telephone. Be sure to explain this list to each family member and babysitters.

○ Check your heating system for carbon monoxide leaks and install carbon monoxide detectors where needed. If you already have a detector, check its batteries.

○ Place a rechargeable flash-light near your bed.

○ If you have children, in-spect your home for poten-tial dangers and childproof it. Place covers on all elec-trical outlets. Make sure cleaners, medicines and other poisonous substances are in the proper containers and stored well out of reach.

○ Check your clothes dryer hose to prevent lint buildup.

○ Label your circuit breakers with an ink pen so you are pre-pared for future power outages.

○ Check for frayed electrical cords on appliances and lamps.

○ If you have a fireplace, schedule a yearly inspection.

○ Create an emergency kit for your family. Include candles, matches, first aid supplies, batteries, flashlight and a blan-ket.

○ Talk to your children about safety. Teach them: how to lock the doors; who to call for help; first aid for a cut; and what to do if they get lost. Contact your local law enforcement for an ID kit. This includes fingerprints, a DNA sample, and personal information.

○ Plan a family meeting to go over all safety rules with your family. Let children ask any questions they want.

TIPS:

- Be aware of the people your children spend time with—babysitters, neighbors, family members of their friends. Talk to them about these people and always keep the lines of communication open so they will come to you if they feel uncomfortable or scared.

- Don't run electrical cords under carpet.

- Don't run your dryer while you are not home.

- Don't overload outlets.

- Adding dead bolts to your exterior doors can help increase the security of your house.

- Clean your clothes dryer's lint filter before each use.

- Don't leave throw rugs at the top of your staircase.

- Be very careful about where you hide a spare key to your home. Your spot may be too obvious.

- Begin replacing the regular incandescent light bulbs in your home with more energy-efficient bulbs.

NOTES:

_____

_____

_____

_____

_____

_____

ONCE A MONTH

◯ Test smoke alarms.

EVERY 3–6 MONTHS

◯ Revisit the fire escape plan with your family.

◯ Change batteries in smoke alarms and carbon monoxide detectors. A good way to remember this is to change the batteries every spring and fall when you change your clocks for daylight savings time.

◯ Change heating, ventilation and air conditioning (HVAC) filters.

◯ Flush your water heaters.

◯ Check your clothes dryer hose for lint buildup.

ONCE A YEAR

◯ Schedule an inspection for your fireplace or furnace.

◯ Check your fire extinguishers.

◯ Check swing sets for loose screws and rust.

Organize After a Loss

We don't like to think about mortality, but it is a reality we all must endure someday. The most important thing to do when reorganizing after a loss is to wait until you are truly ready to deal with the organizing process. There are many stages of grief. One is called reorganization. It usually occurs eighteen to twenty-four months after the loss. During this stage you may notice feelings such as better decision-making and more interest in looking toward the future. Don't beat yourself up if you are noticing this stage earlier than eighteen months or later than twenty-four months—that is just the average. When you do reach this stage, you will most likely be more prepared for organizing. Give yourself permission to let your loved one's possessions go—it is okay. The items that are really hard to part with can go to a great new home where a new person can enjoy them. It is much better to pass them on with love to someone who will use and appreciate them than to keep them out of guilt.

THIS WEEK'S GOALS:

○ Set aside a room or an open space for sorting your loved one's items into categories.

○ Sort and divide items into these categories:
  - *Toss*
  - *Donate*
  - *Sell*
  - *Pass on to a family member/friend*
  - *Keep*
  - *Not sure*

○ Remove the Toss pile and the Donate pile from the home. If you are reorganizing after the loss of a parent, have your

○ siblings check the Toss and Donate piles for anything they want to keep.

○ Invite family and friends to come over and pick up items you think they may want. You should probably do this before you start selling anything in case there is a loved one who is attached to a certain item.

○ Decide what you will do with the Sell pile. You may want to:
- *Have an estate sale*
- *Have a garage sale*
- *Sell the items on the Internet*

○ Pack up the Not Sure pile if you are not ready to get rid of the items. Store them in labeled containers. It may be easier to decide what to do with these items as time goes on. Check the Internet for websites that offer archival-quality storage containers. Give yourself a deadline to make your decision and write that date on the box.

NOTES:

_____

_____

_____

_____

_____

_____

TIPS:

- After you lose a parent, you may move through your grief faster than your siblings. If you are ready to reorganize before they even want to think about it, you can avoid tension by simply identifying the objects you want to keep and putting the rest into storage (possibly a rental unit) until everyone is ready to deal with the belongings.

- Ask friends, family or neighbors for help when you need it. Many people would love to give their time to help but are not sure if they are needed or wanted during this personal time.

- Explain to children what is happening within the family during this stage of life. Take time to listen to their concerns and feelings.

- Go at a pace that works for you. Sorting and organizing a deceased loved one's belongings can be a very emotionally draining experience. Don't be hard on yourself if you move slowly. This is a huge responsibility.

- Check your loved one's planner or schedule and call to cancel any appointments that have been made.

- It is normal for feelings of sadness, despair and even anger to come up during this process. If it gets to be too much in one day, take a break and start again another day.

- Consider hiring a professional organizer to help make this task easier. He or she can give you tips for making decisions and moving forward until the job is complete.

- Remember that ultimately memories are in our minds, not in things.

Organize Your Routines

Organize Your Morning Routine

Are your mornings filled with arguments, impatience, stress and aggravation? No one likes to start off his or her day in a hurried frenzy. If you start of your day overwhelmed, stressed out and late, chances are you will expect the rest of your day to continue the same way. And expecting it will most likely make it happen.

I used to dread getting my daughter up for school. It would take about four tries, and she would wake up groggy, dragging her feet, and I would get impatient and frustrated. So, when she turned seven, I gave my daughter her own alarm clock. Our mornings run so much smoother now because by the time I go up to her room she is up, dressed (we put her clothes out the night before) and ready for breakfast.

Remember, it takes about twenty-eight days to form a new habit. Take your new routine one day at a time during this period. If you need to wake up earlier to give yourself a better start to the day, go to bed earlier. It will be harder to wake up if you are missing sleep. You'll be cranky and more likely to throw in the towel.

THIS WEEK'S GOALS:

○ Have each family member make a list of everything he or she needs to do in the morning. Include all chores, grooming habits, breakfast and inspirational time. If there is something someone would like to do, but isn't currently doing (such as exercise or spend time in quite mediation), add it to the list.

○ Estimate how long each task takes to complete and write that amount of time next to the activity. Have each per-

My routine evolved over many months by adding a new habit every few weeks. That is what I needed to make the habits stick.

—MARLA CILLEY, THE FLYLADY

son tally up the total time needed to complete his or her list.

○ Evaluate the lists. Does everything need to be done in the morning? Are there things that could be done the night before that would make it faster and easier in the morning? Showering, making lunches, packing up backpacks or briefcases and selecting an outfit are all things that can be done the night before. If mornings are a struggle, don't over schedule them. Some people can only handle, the bare minimum of getting dressed, eating breakfast and walking out the door. If this is you (or someone in your family), don't fight it. Do everything you can the night before so you don't have to worry about it in the morning.

○ Organize your final list so it is efficient and makes sense to you. Keep related items together. Do all your grooming, then eat breakfast, then do all your chores. Have each family member post this list by his or her bed or in the bathroom if needed.

○ Re-tally the time it takes to complete your routine if you have removed items from it. What time do you wake up? What time do you have to leave the house? Are you giving yourself enough time to finish your routine? Remember, people are pretty conservative when they estimate time, and you probably move slower in the morning, so tack on an extra ten minutes so you are not rushed. Readjust your wake up time if needed. And readjust your bedtime if you change your wake up time.

○ Set up a family Launch Pad. This is a designated home for the items each family member needs for the day. See list below for examples of Launch Pad items for kids and adults.

○ Create specific homes for each item stored in the Launch Pad. You can use cubbies, hooks or baskets. Just be sure the system is easy for everyone to use. See Organize Your Entryway or Mudroom (Week 20) for more ideas.

○ Establish the rules of the Launch Pad: Each family member must contain his or her items in only his or her pad. All items must be returned to the pad when a person comes home. Post these rules until everyone has them down.

○ Laminate a morning routine checklist and post it in your Launch Pad area to help the routine go more smoothly.

○ If you want to improve your life, improve your morning routine. Come up with 5-10 tasks you can do each morning that will make the biggest impact on your success in life.

TIPS:

- If you are a coffee drinker, prepare the coffee pot and set the timer the night before.

💲 Save time and money by making your own coffee in the morning instead of stopping at the nearest coffee shop.

- Consider reading from your favorite spiritual guide or motivational book first thing in the morning. This can get your day off on the right foot.

LAUNCH PAD CHECKLIST

○ Launch Pad checklist for kids:

    __ Lunch

    __ Books

    __ Signed permission slips

    __ Sports equipment

    __ Musical instrument

    __ Weather gear

    __ Library books

○ Launch Pad checklist for adults:

    __ Keys

    __ Bank deposit

    __ Turn lights and appliances off

    __ Dinner out to thaw

    __ Purse/wallet, briefcase

    __ Things to return

    __ Security system on

NOTES:

Organize Your Evening Routine

The end of the day is an important time. Usually this is the time when a hectic work or school day is over and it is time to relax and reconnect with ourselves and our family. Take some time to rest before you start your evening routine. Change out of your work clothes and into some comfortable clothing to help you relax. Then take ten minutes to decompress either by yourself or with your children, your spouse, or your pet. Use this time to let go of your worries and stressors for the day. Your workday is over. You accomplished what you could with it. Worrying about leftover tasks won't get them done any sooner. You can tackle them fresh tomorrow. You are off the clock—don't steal free time from yourself by worrying about work at home. Get in the habit of doing something that calms you before bed.

THIS WEEK'S GOALS:

○ Have each family member make a list of everything he or she needs or wants to do each evening—the time between arriving home at the end of the day and bedtime. Include all chores, meal preparation, homework, grooming habits and relaxing. Be sure to include anything that you moved from your morning routine to your evening routine. If there is something someone would like to do, but isn't currently doing, add it to the list.

○ Estimate how long each task takes to complete and write that amount of time next to the activity.

○ Set a consistent dinner time and pledge to stick to this meal time as an entire family. It should be a realistic goal. Make

It's up to us to choose how we will spend our lives. Displace the boring, routine, nonproductive activities you're engaging in with exciting, vibrant opportunities that will give your life greater meaning.

—**HAROLD TAYLOR**

sure you have enough time to prepare a nutritious meal and everyone will be available. Of course, there will be nights when you just can't make dinner at this time, but aim to meet this schedule 80 percent of the time.

○ Set a consistent bedtime for each family member—including adults. You'll be much more rested and enjoy better sleep if you keep a consistent bedtime and waking time. Let your waking time determine your bedtime to ensure you are getting enough sleep. Most adults need seven to eight solid hours a night. Children need at least eight hours, and probably more the younger they are.

○ With the family dinner time and bedtime established, allow each family member to arrange the rest of his or her evening activities in a way that works for him or her. Some children may want to do homework as soon as they get home while others may want to wait until after dinner.

○ Build in some downtime at the beginning of the routine so children have a chance to relax after school. Then try to finish the rest of the routine before the additional downtime so your child doesn't get distracted or lose energy.

○ Have each person list evening activities that occur only once or twice a week. These are extracurricular activities such as music lessons, athletic or dance lessons, religious meetings and exercise classes. Adapt your routine to include these activities and include them on the family calendar.

TIPS:

- Post a copy of the evening routine in your child's bedroom or the kitchen if it will help him remember what he needs to accomplish. Use pictures if he is young.

- Limit the number of extracurricular activities your family is involved in. If you have something planned each night of the week, you'll have little downtime and you will struggle with family dinner times. When you place limits, you actually allow your children to enjoy their childhoods more, because they'll have more free playtime and they will only participate in activities that they truly love.

- Designate some time just for yourself or your family during these hours. Turn off your cell phone and the television and reconnect.

- Take the time to ask family members about their day. I ask my kids, "What was the best part of your day" and "What was the worst part?"

- Selecting your children's outfits the night before saves a lot of time in the morning and helps them dress themselves.

- Make dinner a team effort so that you are all together in the kitchen. Kids can help set the table or pitch in with the cooking. Mom and Dad can split the responsibilities. The best rule my husband and I ever established early on was whoever cooks the meal doesn't have to clean up after it.

- Give your children a peaceful place to do their homework. Turn off the television during this time so they can concentrate.

- If your child likes to read in bed, install a timer on her light and set it to go off at her designated bedtime.

EVENING ROUTINE CHECKLIST

Here's an example of what your child's evening routine could look like. Remember, a child's energy level will decrease as the evening progresses. Trying to do everything right before bed will stimulate the child and make it difficult to go to sleep. Plan something relaxing right before bed.

__ Arrive home, put items away in Launch Pad

__ Snack

__ Play for thirty minutes to an hour

__ Do homework (thirty minute to an hour, depending on age)

__ Do chores, including pet care, cleaning tasks, and helping with dinner (twenty minutes)

__ Family dinner (thirty minutes)

__ Round up all items needed for the next day, place in Launch Pad (ten minutes)

__ Help make lunch for the next day (ten minutes)

__ Bathe (ten minutes)

__ Pick out clothes for the next day (five minutes)

__ Family downtime (this can include game night, play-time, reading, watching television)

__ Brush teeth

__ Go to bed

NOTES:

_____

_____

_____

_____

Organize Your Grocery Shopping

The secret to making a trip to the grocery store as stress-free and painless as possible is one word: Plan! Planning ahead will not only save you time from wandering aimlessly from aisle to aisle wondering what you should buy this week, it will also save you a ton of money. You can get in and out of the store in less than forty-five minutes, and you won't get home and realize you're missing half of the ingredients you need to make dinner.

Organizing your grocery shopping goes hand and hand with keeping your pantry and refrigerator organized so make sure you have read Weeks 24 & 25 beore you read this chapter. I try not to grocery shop more then three times a month. This not only saves me time but it helps save food from going to waste. We really try to use up what we have already purchased in the refrigerator before buying more.

THIS WEEK'S GOALS:

○ Schedule time on your calendar to make a list of everything you regularly buy at the grocery store. Check your pantry and refrigerator so you don't forget anything. Be sure to include toiletries and other non-food items you regularly purchase. Type this list on a computer and print it out or use the note sections on your phone like I do. Take it with you the next time you go to the store. As you shop, write the aisle number next to each item. When you return home, organize the list by aisle. It sounds tedious, but this will save you tons of time on future shopping trips.

○ Print copies of your master list and keep a list on the side of your refrigerator or on the inside of a cupboard door at all times.

○ Explain to your family members that they need to mark an item on the list when they see that the item is running low or when they use the last of the item. Also explain that if a family member has a special request, he or she can write it on the list. If an item is frequently added to the list, update your master list and print out new copies to include the item.

○ Before you go to the grocery store, quickly organize your refrigerator (Week 25) and your pantry (Week 24). While doing this, scan for items you are missing for the meals you have planned. Record these items on the current grocery list print out.

○ Use your meal plan (see Week 56) to round out your grocery list. Double-check the recipes to make sure you don't forget any necessary ingredients before you go grocery shopping.

TIPS:

- There are so many apps that will help you organize your grocery shopping. Do a quick Google search to find the one that works best for your family.

- 💲 Always check your store's sales fliers while making your grocery list. You may find deals worth stocking up on.

- Shopping at the same store saves you lots of time. You'll know exactly where everything is and won't have to waste time learning the different layouts of various stores.

- Try to grocery shop during the times your store is least busy. This is typically on weekdays, especially early in the morning or at meal times (just don't shop while you're hungry).

- Maximize your savings by using your coupons when products are on sale at their lowest price point. Products reach this point about every twelve weeks. When the sale hits, stock up. There are tons of websites that make it easy for you to match up coupons with sales items. These sites give you a breakdown of what to buy, and when and where to buy it.

- Keep your pantry, cupboards and spare closets clean and organized so you can effectively stockpile nonperishables and take full advantage of sales and coupons. Organized food storage lets you know exactly what you have and makes it easy to find the food you are looking for when you are cooking.

- Many stores will let you use their store coupon and a manufacturer's coupon at the same time on the same product.

- Be aware of your favorite store's reward policies and use them to your advantage. Some stores give gifts cards for buying particular products while others give you dollars off on the end of your receipt to use on your next purchase. Check your favorite stores' websites to learn all the details of their programs.

NOTES:

_____

_____

_____

_____

_____

_____

_____

GROCERY SHOPPING CHECKLIST

This is a general grocery list. Add specifics to it to create your master grocery list.

Produce

Vegetables_____

Fruit_____

Meat/fish/poultr_____

Canned Goods

Soups _____

Beans _____

Vegetables_____

Sauces/condiment_____

Baking Goods

Flour

Sugar

Baking soda

Salt

Spices_____

Pasta/rice/mixes _____

Bread

Cereal/breakfast_____

Cleaning/laundry products_____

Paper products_____

Personal care_____

Baby/pet product_____

Snacks _____

Beverages_____

Frozen foods _____

Dairy_____

Organize Your Meal Planning

I have to admit meal planning is one of my least favorite things to organize. I think the part I hate the most is coming up with the recipes. Recently, I have been so frustrated with this part of my week that I set out to research tools that may help me, and I discovered great websites full of ideas for fresh, healthy meals that kids and adults love.

If you plan your meals ahead of time and use your plan to make your grocery list, you will save money because you will use up everything you purchase instead of letting some food go bad. You also will be less likely to go out to eat.

One easy approach is to have theme days. This gives you enough structure that you can quickly find a recipe, but enough flexibility that you don't have to eat the exact same meals every week. If your family has a favorite meal, you may be able to get away with serving it every week. My kids decided on their own that they love tacos so much that they want us to have them every week, and we have declared Tuesday night taco night.

THIS WEEK'S GOALS:

○ Make a list of your family's favorite meals and get input from each family member.

○ Go through your cookbooks and recipe collection and list out the ones you can easily prepare and that your family enjoyed eating. Note the page number and cookbook title on the list so you can quickly find it again. Add this to your family's list of favorites.

○ As you go through your cookbook, write down recipes you have not made but would like to try, and place them in list. If need be, separate this list into everyday meals and special

Food, love, career, and
mothers, the four major
guilt groups.

—CATHY GUISEWITE

occasion meals. Everyday meals involve mostly stock ingredients and shouldn't take more than an hour to prepare and cook (unless you're using a slow cooker). Special occasion meals involve more exotic or expensive ingredients and take longer to prepare.

○ Schedule time on your calendar for meal planning. Try to block out the same time each week so you stick to it. You can meal plan while you watch TV or listen to your favorite music.

○ Use the recipe lists you compiled to plan your meals. Each week, prepare one or two family favorites, one or two staples and try one new recipe. The new recipes may become favorites.

○ Build simple structure into your meal plan. A friend of mine recently told me that she follows a simple schedule like this:
  Monday: chicken
  Tuesday: beef
  Wednesday: open
  Thursday: open
  Friday: order in or eat out
  Saturday: snack night
  Sunday: soup night

○ Get your family involved. If you have teenage children, have them cook dinner one night per week. Try to make it the same night each week. Let them select what meal they prepare, but encourage them to try a variety of recipes so they get experience working with different types of foods and various cooking techniques. This teaches them valuable life skills and takes some of the burden off of you. Be on hand to coach them through the first month or two (and any new or challenging recipes after that). It can be great bonding time with your child. This goal should be applied to both daughters and sons because every responsible adult needs to know how to cook a proper meal.

TIPS:

- On the days that you work, opt for the quick and easy recipes. Save the more tedious ones for the days you have off.

- Extend the life of food products by refrigerating them whenever possible. This is a good idea for bread.

- $ Save some money and simplify by declaring one night a week as leftover night. Any leftovers count!

- $ Before you meal plan, take stock of your pantry and refrigerator and select recipes that use the food that you already have on hand.

- Multi-task while preparing dinner. Use the cooking time to set the table, empty or load the dishwasher and quickly clean around the kitchen. Better yet, have another family member get the table set while you are cooking.

- When possible double a recipe and freeze the extra portions for a quick future meal.

- My go to for receipes will always be Pinterest. Check out my receipe boarch under: Organize Now.

- Make it a rule that everyone must eat the same meal. Don't make different meals for different family members. Once you start this they will expect it!

ONCE A MONTH

○ Take some time to check websites and magazines for coupons.

EVERY 3–6 MONTHS

○ Skip a week of grocery shopping and use up as many of the ingredients you already have in the house as possible. This helps you clean out your pantry and freezer.

ONCE A YEAR

○ Renew any memberships you have to members-only grocery stores.

NOTES:

_____

_____

_____

_____

_____

_____

_____

_____

_____

_____

_____

_____

_____

index